# Asbestos Bankruptcy Trusts and Tort Compensation

Lloyd Dixon, Geoffrey McGovern

RAND INSTITUTE FOR CIVIL JUSTICE

The research described in this monograph was conducted by the RAND Institute for Civil Justice, a unit of the RAND Corporation. This research was supported by a coalition of asbestos defendants and insurers and by the RAND Institute for Civil Justice.

**Library of Congress Cataloging-in-Publication Data**

Dixon, Lloyd S.
Asbestos bankruptcy trusts and tort compensation / Lloyd Dixon, Geoffrey McGovern.
p. cm.
Includes bibliographical references.
ISBN 978-0-8330-5834-8 (pbk. : alk. paper)
1. Bankruptcy trustees—United States. 2. Compensation (Law)—United States. 3. Toxic torts—United States. 4. Personal injuries—United States. 5. Trusts and trustees—United States. 6. Asbestos—Law and legislation—United States. I. McGovern, Geoffrey. II. Title.

KF1530.R3D594 2011
346.7307'8—dc23

2011031315



Published 2011 by the RAND Corporation
1776 Main Street, P.O. Box 2138, Santa Monica, CA 90407-2138
1200 South Hayes Street, Arlington, VA 22202-5050
4570 Fifth Avenue, Suite 600, Pittsburgh, PA 15213-2665
RAND URL: http://www.rand.org/
To order RAND documents or to obtain additional information, contact
Distribution Services: Telephone: (310) 451-7002;
Fax: (310) 451-6915; Email: order@rand.org

# Preface

Over the past ten years, payments by asbestos bankruptcy trusts have played an increasingly important role in compensating asbestos injuries and have become a matter of contention between plaintiff and defense attorneys. At issue is how tort cases take into consideration compensation paid by trusts and the evidence submitted in trust claim forms. This monograph examines how such evidence and compensation are addressed by state laws and taken into consideration during court proceedings. It also examines how the establishment of the trusts potentially affects total plaintiff compensation, payments by defendants that remain solvent, and the compensation available to future, as compared to current, plaintiffs.

This monograph is part of a larger research project on asbestos bankruptcy trusts. A previous report provides an overview of the trusts and compiles publicly available information on the assets, outlays, claim-approval criteria, and governing boards of the leading trusts.[1]

This research was supported by the RAND Institute for Civil Justice (ICJ) and by contributions from the following asbestos defendants and insurers: Bondex International; Coalition for Litigation Justice; Crane Company; Dow Chemical Company; E. I. DuPont De Nemours and Company; Exxon Mobil Corporation; Garrison Litigation Management Group; General Electric Company; Georgia-Pacific; The Hartford; Herzfeld and Rubin; Owens-Illinois General; Saint-Gobain Corporation; Swanson, Martin and Bell; and the U.S. Chamber of Commerce. The views expressed in this monograph are those of the authors and do not necessarily reflect those of the research sponsors.

## The RAND Institute for Civil Justice

The mission of ICJ is to improve private and public decisionmaking on civil legal issues by supplying policymakers and the public with the results of objective, empirically based, analytic research. ICJ facilitates change in the civil justice system by analyzing

---

[1] Dixon, McGovern, and Coombe, 2010.

trends and outcomes, identifying and evaluating policy options, and bringing together representatives of different interests to debate alternative solutions to policy problems. ICJ builds on a long tradition of RAND research characterized by an interdisciplinary, empirical approach to public policy issues and rigorous standards of quality, objectivity, and independence.

ICJ research is supported by pooled grants from corporations, trade and professional associations, and individuals; by government grants and contracts; and by private foundations. ICJ disseminates its work widely to the legal, business, and research communities and to the general public. In accordance with RAND policy, all ICJ research products are subject to peer review before publication. ICJ publications do not necessarily reflect the opinions or policies of the research sponsors or of the ICJ Board of Overseers.

Information about ICJ is available online (http://www.rand.org/icj.html). Inquiries about research projects should be sent to the following address:

James Dertouzos, Director
RAND Institute for Civil Justice
1776 Main Street
P.O. Box 2138
Santa Monica, CA 90407-2138
310-393-0411 x7476
Fax: 310-451-6979
James_Dertouzos@rand.org

Questions and comments about this monograph should be sent to Lloyd Dixon (Lloyd_Dixon@rand.org).

# Contents

**Preface** ... iii
**Figures** ... vii
**Tables** ... ix
**Summary** ... xi
**Acknowledgments** ... xvii
**Abbreviations** ... xix

CHAPTER ONE
**Introduction** ... 1
Background on Asbestos Litigation and the Rise of the Trusts ... 2
Linkages Between Trusts and Tort Cases ... 3
Information Linkage ... 6
Setoff Linkage ... 6
Indirect Claim Linkage ... 6
Trust Payment Limitation Linkage ... 6
Defendant and Plaintiff Concerns About Trusts' Roles in Tort Litigation ... 7
Focus and Methods of This Monograph ... 8
Organization of This Monograph ... 9

CHAPTER TWO
**Linkages Between the Trusts and Tort Cases in Six States** ... 11
Liability Regime ... 12
Liability Standard ... 12
Assigning Fault to Trusts or Bankrupt Firms ... 14
The Information Linkage: Filing, Disclosure, and Timing of Trust Claims ... 17
Disclosure of Trust Claim Forms ... 17
Timing of Trust Claim Submissions ... 18
The Setoff Linkage: Setoffs for Trust Payments ... 20
The Indirect Claim Linkage: Indirect Trust Claims ... 23
Trust Payment Limitation Linkage: Trust Limits on Payments to Direct Claimants ... 26
Extent to Which Trusts Are Treated Differently from Solvent Defendants ... 28

Summary of Linkages Between Trusts and Tort Cases ........ 29
Information Linkage ........ 29
Setoff Linkage ........ 30
Indirect Trust Claim Linkage ........ 30
Trust Payment Limitation Linkage ........ 30
Conclusion ........ 31

CHAPTER THREE
**Potential Effects That Trusts Can Have on Total Plaintiff Compensation and Payments by Defendants That Remain Solvent** ........ 33
Range of Potential Effects ........ 33
Effects in States with Joint-and-Several Liability ........ 36
West Virginia ........ 37
Illinois ........ 39
Pennsylvania ........ 39
Effects in States with Several Liability ........ 41
California ........ 41
New York ........ 44
Texas ........ 45
Synthesis of Findings on the Potential Effects of Trusts ........ 46
Potential Effects on Plaintiff Compensation and Defendant Payments ........ 46
Importance of Evidence on Exposure to the Products and Practices of Bankrupt Firms ........ 49

CHAPTER FOUR
**Conclusion** ........ 55
Implications of the Findings ........ 55
Limitations and Next Steps ........ 58

APPENDIXES
A. **Background on Liability Standards** ........ 59
B. **Liability Rules and Court Procedures Relevant to Asbestos Bankruptcy Trusts in Six States** ........ 61

**Glossary** ........ 83
**References** ........ 85

# Figures

1.1. Potential Linkages Between Different Sources of Asbestos Compensation........ 4
3.1. Range of Outcomes Possible in the Joint-and-Several-Liability States Compared with Those in the Several-Liability States .............................. 50

# Tables


2.1. Liability Standards.......... 12
2.2. Assigning Fault to Bankrupt Firms or Trusts .......... 14
2.3. Filing and Discovery Requirements for Trust Claim Forms .......... 18
2.4. Setoffs for Pre-Verdict Trust Payments.......... 21
3.1. Different Cases for the Change in Plaintiff Compensation Due to Trusts .......... 35
3.2. Example of No Change in Total Plaintiff Compensation in West Virginia .......... 38
3.3. Example of No Change in Total Plaintiff Compensation in Pennsylvania.......... 40
3.4. Example of a Decrease in Total Plaintiff Compensation for Noneconomic Damages in California .......... 42
3.5. Example of an Increase in Total Plaintiff Compensation for Noneconomic Damages in California .......... 43
3.6. Example of an Increase in Total Plaintiff Compensation for Noneconomic Damages in New York .......... 44
3.7. Example of a Decrease in Total Plaintiff Compensation for Noneconomic Damages in New York .......... 46
3.8. Example of an Increase in Total Plaintiff Compensation in Texas .......... 47
3.9. Example of a Decrease of Total Plaintiff Compensation in Texas .......... 48
3.10. Summary of Potential Effects of the Trusts in the Six States Examined.......... 48

# Summary

Asbestos litigation in the United States began in the 1970s and grew rapidly in the subsequent decades. By 2002, an estimated 730,000 people had filed asbestos-related lawsuits, and $49 billion had been paid in compensation. As past and expected future payments mounted, many of the primary asbestos defendants filed for reorganization under U.S. bankruptcy law. At that point, all lawsuits against them were halted. After negotiations with creditors, including asbestos claimants represented by their counsel, many companies established an independent asbestos personal injury trust to pay asbestos claims.

Over the past 30 years, 56 asbestos personal injury trusts have been set up on behalf of companies that have filed for reorganization. The largest 26 trusts paid $10.9 billion on 2.4 million claims through 2008. Trust outlays have grown rapidly since 2005, reaching $3.3 billion in 2008. Given these sizable assets, and the great reservoir of future asbestos personal injury claims, both plaintiffs and solvent defendants have a great deal at stake with regard to how trusts enter into the determination of tort awards. At issue is whether a lack of coordination between the trusts and the tort system allows plaintiffs to, in effect, recover once in the tort system and then again from the trusts. Similarly at issue is whether the payments by solvent defendants are being properly adjusted to account for the compensation available from the trusts. Higher trust payments to current plaintiffs mean fewer trust resources for future plaintiffs, so also of concern is whether a lack of coordination between trusts and the tort system advantages today's plaintiffs relative to future plaintiffs.

This study examines the interactions between the trusts and the tort system. Although we were not able to determine what actually occurs in practice—data on plaintiff compensation over time are simply not available—we were able to determine how trust payments are factored into tort awards in different states and how trust payments can potentially affect total plaintiff compensation (from the trusts and the tort system) and payments by solvent defendants.

## Approach

Our analysis considers this issue by examining all the steps in the process for obtaining compensation and then identifying where the trusts and court cases interact in this process. We identify four potential opportunities for interaction—or linkages:

- *The information linkage.* We examine whether the claim forms and supporting exposure evidence submitted to trusts are provided to tort defendants. Because claim disclosure requirements are of little import if no claims have been filed, we also investigate whether there are state requirements on when a trust claim must be filed during a tort case.
- *The setoff linkage.* In tort litigation, defendants often settle before trial, and, because those settlements are intended to compensate the plaintiff for the alleged harm, states often allow credit to be given to the defendants found liable for money the plaintiff has already received. We examine whether these "setoffs" are available for pre-verdict trust payments in asbestos cases.
- *The indirect claim linkage.* Indirect personal injury claims are claims for compensation filed with a trust by a party other than the original asbestos claimant (the direct claimant). For example, a tort defendant that pays the full judgment might gain the right to pursue an indirect claim. If successful, the indirect claimant would recover the same amount that the direct claimant would have been paid.
- *The trust payment limitation linkage.* Restrictions in the governing documents of some trusts condition trust payments on outcomes in the tort system. For example, some trusts will not pay a direct claim if another party has satisfied the trust's liability in full. This and other conditions provide feedback between the trusts and the tort case, affecting both plaintiff compensation from trust and tort combined and payments by defendants that remain solvent.

We chose six states that vary a great deal in their statutory laws and court rules. We selected California, Illinois, New York, Pennsylvania, and Texas because they have a history of a large number of asbestos filings, and we included a sixth state, West Virginia, because of its innovative approach to dealing with the trusts. California, New York, and Texas have adopted some form of several liability, which means that a defendant's liability in these states can be limited to the portion of the harm for which it is responsible, as determined in trial. Illinois, Pennsylvania, and West Virginia, on the other hand, have *joint-and-several liability*, which means that the plaintiff can recover the entire judgment from any one of the liable defendants.[1] The difference between

---

[1] Liability for asbestos injuries has recently changed in Pennsylvania and is now several, subject to some exceptions. The change does not apply to cases in which the plaintiff knew or should have known prior to June 28, 2011, that he or she was injured. The analysis in this monograph applies to Pennsylvania cases subject to this *prior* liability regime.

these two liability regimes, it turns out, has a strong effect on the interactions between the trust and tort system and ultimately on compensation.

Because we did not have actual data for calculating compensation, we engaged in the following thought experiment. First, assume that all potential defendants in an asbestos personal injury case are solvent and that the jury returns a verdict in favor of the plaintiff, allocating liability to the defendants in accordance with the relevant state laws (the pre-reorganization scenario). Now consider the same plaintiff facing the same jury in the same state, but with some of the defendants reorganized and trusts up and running in their place (the post-reorganization scenario). Further assume that the jury verdict is the same in both scenarios and that the combined trust payments are less than the combined payments in the pre-reorganization scenario of defendants that will be reorganized. We use this hypothetical situation to explore the potential impact that the trusts could have on total plaintiff compensation and on payments by defendants that remain solvent. The effect of the trusts on total plaintiff compensation is the amount received in the post-reorganization scenario less the amount received in the pre-reorganization scenario. The trusts' effect on payments by defendants that remain solvent is defined similarly.[2]

We drew on experts for information about the ways in which the trusts and tort system relate to each other in different states. We conducted individual and group interviews with representatives of the plaintiff bar, defense bar, and the trusts, all on a confidential basis. For each of the six states, we sought and obtained cooperation of plaintiff and defense attorneys who practiced in the state. Overall, we interviewed 20 defense attorneys, 11 plaintiff attorneys, and six trust managers or counsel, some of them multiple times. We also reviewed relevant state statutes, court rules, and controlling appellate opinions.

## Results: Linkages Between Trusts and Tort Cases

We found a great deal of variation across states with regard to how trust compensation enters into the determination of tort awards. This variation is caused by differences in liability standards and practices that determine when trust claims must be filed during a tort case, whether setoffs are allowed, and whether fault can be assigned to bankrupt firms.

### Information Sharing

Courts in the six states typically require the disclosure of the claim forms for trust claims that have been filed. However, plaintiffs are seldom required to file trust claims

---

[2] We do not consider the transition period between the time a firm files for reorganization and when a trust is paying claims in its place. We thus focus on the longer-run impact that the replacement of solvent defendants by trusts can have.

before trial. Courts in New York City and in Montgomery County, Pennsylvania, require all trust claims to be filed before trial, but there is no such requirement in the other jurisdictions we examined. When trust claims are not filed prior to trial, defendants will not receive setoffs for trust payments and might not have the information they need to assign fault to bankrupt firms or to pursue indirect trust claims postjudgment.

### Setoffs

Four of the states examined (Illinois, New York, Texas, and West Virginia) allow setoffs for all pre-verdict trust payments; Pennsylvania and California do not. Defendants in California do not receive setoffs for that portion of a trust payment the court attributes to noneconomic damages. However, the same is true for noneconomic damage settlements by solvent parties. In Pennsylvania, setoffs have typically been allowed only when the trust has been assigned fault, but, in contrast to solvent parties, trusts typically cannot be assigned fault in Pennsylvania. Pennsylvania law regarding setoffs for trust payments, however, might be changing.

### Indirect Trust Claims

In joint-and-several-liability states, the verdict defendant will typically be able to recover from a trust if it fully satisfies the judgment and meets the exposure and other requirements that apply to the direct claimant. However, the defendant often needs the plaintiff's cooperation to develop the information required to bring a trust claim, and such cooperation is uncertain. When liability is several, a verdict defendant does not cover the liability of other parties and thus will not be able to bring an indirect claim against a trust.

### Limitation on Trust Payments

Provisions at some trusts prohibit payments to direct claimants when the trust's liability has been satisfied by another party and require direct claimants to indemnify the trust for future indirect claims. Such provisions prevent trusts from paying more than once on the same injury and reduce the likelihood that a plaintiff will receive more than the full value of injury. Some trusts, however, do not have such provisions. In any case, our interviews suggest that most trusts are on the lookout for circumstances in which an injured party would receive trust compensation for damages that were covered by another source.

## Results: Effects on Total Plaintiff Compensation and Payments by Solvent Defendants

Our findings indicate that the potential effects of the replacement of once-solvent defendants by trusts are very different in states with joint-and-several liability than in states with several liability.

In states with joint-and-several liability, total plaintiff compensation should not change. That is because of setoffs for pre-verdict trust payments, the availability of indirect claims, and trust provisions that require the direct claimant to indemnify the trust for subsequent indirect payments. In contrast, payments by defendants that remain solvent will likely increase in these states. If all potential claims are brought against the trusts, payment by defendants that remain solvent will increase by the amount that the bankrupt firms would have paid in the pre-reorganization scenario, less the amount covered by the trusts. Such an outcome is consistent with the intent of joint-and-several liability: A plaintiff can recover from any one defendant, and the defendant is responsible for the shares of other defendants that cannot be collected. However, if information on exposure to the bankrupt firms' products and practices is not developed and neither direct nor indirect claims are brought against some trusts, then payments by solvent defendants could increase further. In the extreme, all trust money can be left on the table, and the defendants that remain solvent can be required to cover the entire amount that would have been paid by the bankrupt firms in the pre-reorganization scenario. In other words, the solvent defendants do not receive credit for the compensation available from the trusts.

In several-liability states, the replacement of once-solvent defendants by trusts can cause total plaintiff compensation to increase, decrease, or remain unchanged. Payments by defendants that remain solvent can increase or remain unchanged. Which outcomes occur depends on the extent to which the jury assigns fault to the bankrupt firms in the post-reorganization scenario. If the solvent defendants are successful in persuading the jury to assign the same fault to the bankrupt firms in the pre- and post-reorganization scenarios, then total plaintiff compensation will decrease, and payments by the defendants that remain solvent will remain unchanged. If, on the other hand, the bankrupt firms are assigned less fault than would have been the case in the pre-reorganization scenario, total plaintiff compensation and payments by the defendants that remain solvent can increase. In the extreme, the plaintiff can receive full compensation in the tort system and then receive additional compensation from the trusts. Such an outcome is not consistent with the doctrine in several-liability states that holds defendants responsible for only their share of the fault. Although the additional trust payments benefit current plaintiffs, they can disadvantage future plaintiffs in several-liability states. The additional trust payments deplete trust assets, reducing the amount available for future plaintiffs. If, for example, no solvent party is found liable in a future case, then the plaintiff's only source of compensation will be the trusts. Additional trust payments to current plaintiffs could thus translate into lower total compensation for the future plaintiff.

Our findings underscore the importance of information on exposure to the products and practices of the bankrupt firms in determining the trusts' effects on plaintiff compensation and on payments by defendants that remain solvent. There is a great deal of dispute between plaintiff and defense attorneys over who is responsible for developing evidence on the products and practices of bankrupt firms. Plaintiffs' attorneys argue that defense attorneys can use discovery tools to uncover exposure information. Defense attorneys respond that plaintiffs' attorneys can influence the exposures plaintiffs recall during the court case and that, without plaintiff cooperation, they will not succeed in assembling the information needed to recover from the trusts. We have not examined the dynamics of the discovery process in this study. We note, however, that the stakes regarding the development of this information are greater for both plaintiffs and solvent defendants in states with several liability than they are in states with joint-and-several liability—a factor that could create different incentives to investigate (or to not investigate) exposure information.

Some states have addressed the disputes between plaintiffs and defendants regarding the investigation and filing of trust claims. Plaintiffs in New York City are required to file all trust claims at least 90 days before trial, and West Virginia plaintiffs are required to complete a good-faith investigation of all trust claims no later than 120 days before trial. These rules have the potential to significantly affect outcomes for plaintiffs and the defendants that remain solvent.

## Conclusion

In summary, our analysis identifies a range of potential outcomes for plaintiffs and defendants—outcomes that depend on liability regime, court procedures, and the behaviors of plaintiffs, defendants, and their attorneys. In some cases, the replacement of once-solvent defendants by trusts increases total plaintiff compensation. This increase in total compensation can come at the expense of future plaintiffs. In addition, we have shown that payments by solvent defendants can increase, sometimes by more than the amount of the bankrupt firms' pre-reorganization liability that is not covered by the trusts. We have also identified circumstances under which total plaintiff compensation decreases, as well as circumstances under which total plaintiff compensation and payments by solvent defendants remain unchanged.

Data on total plaintiff compensation over time are needed to determine which outcomes occur in practice. Analysis is also needed to evaluate the performance of the current system and to suggest reforms that will improve outcomes.

# Acknowledgments

We interviewed many of the leading asbestos plaintiff and defense attorneys in the United States during the course of the project, as well as some of the most-knowledgeable lawyers on the procedures and operation of asbestos bankruptcy trusts. This project would not have been possible without their participation.

We would like to thank the following for the time they set aside for interviews, comments on the draft reports, or both: Richard R. Ames at Gibson, Robb and Lindh; David Austern at Claims Resolution Management Corporation; Charles E. Bates at Bates White; Lisa Nathanson Busch at Weitz and Luxenberg; Joseph Cagnoli Jr. at Segal McCambridge Singer and Mahoney; Garland S. Cassada at Robinson Bradshaw and Hinson; Charles E. Finberg at Herzfeld and Rubin; Erich J. Gleber at Segal McCambridge Singer and Mahoney; Steven A. Hart at Segal McCambridge Singer and Mahoney; David K. Hendrickson at Eckert Seamans Cherin and Mellott; Nathan Horne at Segal McCambridge Singer and Mahoney; Elihu Inselbuch at Caplin and Drysdale; Kevin E. Irwin at Keating, Muething and Klekamp; Ken Jacobs at Crane Company; Alice Sacks Johnston at Obermayer Rebmann Maxwell and Hippel; Eliot S. Jubelirer at Schiff Hardin; Steven Kazan at Kazan, McClain, Lyons, Greenwood, and Harley; Peter R. Kelso at Bates White; Jason L. Kennedy at Segal McCambridge Singer and Mahoney; Harold H. Kim at U.S. Chamber Institute for Legal Reform; Peter A. Kraus at Waters and Kraus; Jerry Kristal at Weitz and Luxenberg; Carolyn Kuhl of the Superior Court of California for the County of Los Angeles; John A. LaBoon at Segal McCambridge Singer and Mahoney; Kevin LaFreniere at Hartford Financial Services; Jake S. Lifson at Goehring, Rutter and Boehm; James R. Lynch at Lynch Daskal Emery; William M. Lynch at Liberty Mutual Group; Moshe Maimon at Levy Phillips and Konigsberg; Bruce E. Mattock at Goldberg, Persky, and White; Mark C. Meyer at Goldberg, Persky, and White; Philip Milch at Campbell and Levine; Jennifer Morales at Keating, Muething and Klekamp; Robert W. Phillips at Simmons Browder Gianaris Angelides and Barnerd; Paul D. Rheingold at Rheingold, Valet, Rheingold, Shkolnik and McCartney; David B. Rodes at Goldberg, Persky, and White; Marc Scarcella at Bates White; Charles S. Siegel at Waters and Kraus; Peter J. Strelitz at Segal McCambridge Singer and Mahoney; Robert E. Thackston at Hawkins Parnell Thackston and

Young; Nicholas P. Vari at K&L Gates; and Stacey F. Vernallis at Goehring, Rutter and Boehm.

Others participated in interviews or provided comments on drafts, but they chose not to be identified. The findings in this monograph do not necessarily reflect the views of those who participated in the study.

Detailed and insightful peer reviews were provided by S. Todd Brown at the University at Buffalo Law School and Nicholas M. Pace at RAND. Their comments helped improve the draft considerably.

At RAND, we would like to thank Laura Zakaras for her help in sharpening the summary; Lisa Bernard for skillful editing; Susan M. Gates for moving this document through the RAND quality-assurance process; James N. Dertouzos for providing helpful advice during the course of the project; and Fred Kipperman and Jamie Morikawa for helping secure funding for the project and liaising with project sponsors.

# Abbreviations

| | |
|---|---|
| FIFO | first in, first out |
| ICJ | RAND Institute for Civil Justice |
| PRP | potentially responsible party |
| RTP | responsible third party |
| TDP | trust distribution procedure |

CHAPTER ONE

# Introduction

Over the past 30 years, 56 asbestos personal injury trusts have been set up on behalf of companies that have filed for reorganization under U.S. bankruptcy law.[1] Individuals who allege that they have suffered personal injuries as a result of exposure to asbestos and asbestos-containing products can no longer sue these firms in court but can nevertheless file claims for compensation with their trusts. Trusts are now paying billions of dollars per year to asbestos victims and, as of year-end 2008, reported assets of approximately $30 billion.

At issue is whether a lack of coordination between the trusts and the tort system allows plaintiffs to, in effect, recover once in the tort system and then again from the trusts. Similarly at issue is whether the payments by solvent defendants are being properly adjusted to account for the compensation available from the trusts. Higher trust payments to current plaintiffs will likely mean fewer trust resources for future plaintiffs, so also of concern is whether a lack of coordination between trusts and the tort system advantages today's plaintiffs relative to future plaintiffs.

This monograph examines the linkages between the trusts and tort cases. It describes how trust payments and the potential for such payments are factored into the determination of tort awards. It also explores how trusts potentially affect plaintiff compensation from trust and tort combined and payments by defendants that remain solvent. Our analysis is descriptive rather than normative. It does not assess whether the current linkages between the trusts and tort cases are adequate or whether the trusts' potential impacts on total plaintiff compensation and on payments by defendants that remain solvent are desirable. Rather, it attempts to describe the current linkages between trust and tort and those linkages' potential impacts on total plaintiff compensation and payments by defendants that remain solvent. This monograph builds on a previous RAND Institute for Civil Justice (ICJ) report that provides an

[1] Dixon, McGovern, and Coombe (2010, p. 29) reported that 54 trusts had been set up through mid-2010. Between then and the writing of this monograph in May 2011, asbestos trusts have been established per the confirmations of the Thorpe Insulation Company and General Motors reorganizations.

overview of how trusts are organized and governed, how they operate, and their assets and outlays.[2]

In the remainder of this introductory chapter, we provide background on asbestos personal injury litigation and the rise of the trusts, the potential linkages between trusts and tort cases, defendant and plaintiff concerns about the current situation, and the methods used in our analysis.

## Background on Asbestos Litigation and the Rise of the Trusts

Asbestos was produced and widely used in industrial products throughout the 20th century. The American Academy of Actuaries estimates that as many as 27.5 million Americans used asbestos in the course of their careers.[3] Hundreds of thousands of these workers developed diseases alleged to have been caused or made more severe by asbestos exposure. In 1973, the U.S. Circuit Court of Appeals for the Fifth Circuit issued the first appellate opinion that upheld a product-liability judgment against a manufacturer of asbestos-containing products.[4] This decision began a wave of tort litigation that sought to compensate workers for illnesses caused by asbestos. By 2002, an estimated 730,000 people had filed asbestos-related lawsuits, and $49 billion had been paid in compensation.[5]

As past and expected future payments mounted, many of the primary asbestos defendants filed for reorganization under Section 524(g) of the U.S. Bankruptcy Code. Once a defendant has commenced a bankruptcy case, all lawsuits against the company are halted, and, after negotiations with the company's creditors (including asbestos claimants as represented by their counsel), the company submits a plan for reorganization to the bankruptcy court. The plan often establishes and funds an independent asbestos personal injury trust that then pays asbestos claims on behalf of the bankrupt firm. Any asbestos claim against the bankrupt firm is "channeled" to the trust.

As of March 2011, 96 companies with asbestos liabilities had filed for reorganization, 56 trusts had been established, and additional trusts are in the pipeline. Each trust establishes a schedule of values for asbestos injuries intended to reflect the tort payments made by the bankrupt firm before reorganization.[6] Most trusts do not have sufficient funds to pay every claim in full and, thus, set a payment percentage that is

---

2 Dixon, McGovern, and Coombe, 2010.

3 American Academy of Actuaries, 2007, p. 1.

4 *Borel*, 1973.

5 Carroll et al., 2005, p. xvii.

6 As is discussed in subsequent chapters, there is a great deal of disagreement on how accurately trust injury values reflect the debtor's pre-reorganization payments.

used to determine the actual payment a claimant is offered.[7] The median payment percentage is 25 percent across the 26 trusts examined in Dixon, McGovern, and Coombe (2010, p. xv), with the range running from 1.1 percent to 100 percent. The median amount paid per mesothelioma claim is $41,000 across the same set of trusts, and a plaintiff can receive compensation from multiple trusts.[8] Outlays by the trusts have been substantial. The largest 26 trusts had paid $10.9 billion on 2.4 million claims through 2008. Trust outlays have grown rapidly since 2005, reaching $3.3 billion in 2008. As discussed earlier, trust assets exceeded $30 billion at the end of 2008.[9]

## Linkages Between Trusts and Tort Cases

Asbestos claimants regularly seek to recover from multiple sources, and, when they are successful, their recovery typically comes from more than one entity. It is common, for example, for a plaintiff to receive settlement monies from trusts and solvent companies. Although trials are rare and final judgments rarer still, it is even possible for an asbestos plaintiff to recover from multiple trusts, settle with multiple solvent companies, and collect on a final judgment after winning a trial against multiple solvent defendants.

Every claimant's case will be different, driven by different work histories, exposure to different products, and his or her attorney's strategy for seeking compensation. But, in order to generalize the process and demonstrate the interactions that can take place, we have created a model to depict how the tort system considers payments from trusts and vice versa. Figure 1.1 presents a schematic that depicts the general process. In this figure, we have depicted a stylized diagram of asbestos litigation, focusing on linkages between the different components.

At the first branch of the diagram, a plaintiff faces a choice of whom to pursue. Administrative claims and other presuit settlements, tort claims, and trust claims are the major options. For our purposes, we assume that the plaintiff pursues each of these options.[10]

At the far left of Figure 1.1 are the administrative claims. Administrative claims are a subject that has been little addressed in the literature. Administrative claims

[7] A trust can adjust the payment percentage over time as more information becomes available on the number of claims that will be filed and the performance of its investment portfolio.

[8] The number of trusts from which a claimant can recover will depend on the claimant's work history and exposure to specific asbestos-containing products.

[9] Dixon, McGovern, Coombe, 2010, p. 31.

[10] There are sources of compensation for asbestos claimants other than those shown in Figure 1.1, including workers' compensation, health and life insurance, Medicare, and social security disability payments. There are also rules addressing reimbursement of payment by one source when compensation is subsequently received from another source. For example, regulations requiring that the Medicare program be reimbursed by subsequent insurer payments and tort awards have recently been tightened.

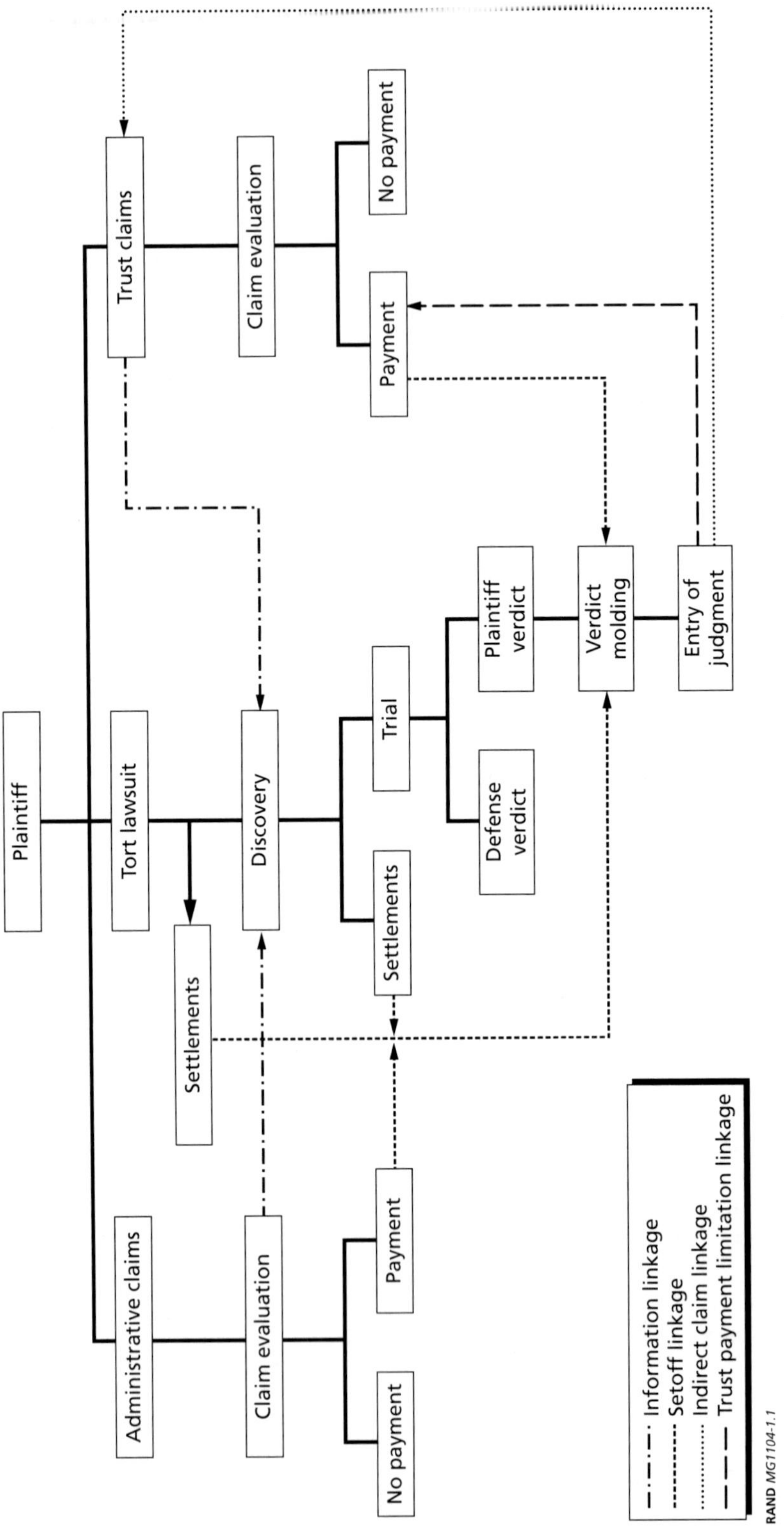


**Figure 1.1**
**Potential Linkages Between Different Sources of Asbestos Compensation**

are typically brought under administrative agreements (a.k.a. matrix deals). Administrative agreements are a type of aggregate settlement reached by plaintiff firms and the manufacturers of asbestos-containing products. For example, a plaintiffs' attorney might have an agreement with a company that any asbestosis claim would be paid a set amount of money, subject to modest evidentiary requirements. This would eliminate the need to negotiate each claim brought to the company and eliminate the need to name the party in the tort case. At the time this monograph was written, there were no readily available data about the number or aggregate value of administrative claims in asbestos litigation. During the course of our study, we heard competing views of the degree to which administrative claims are a part of current asbestos compensation.[11]

The center column of Figure 1.1 represents a simplified trial process and post-trial procedures. Once a tort claim is filed in court and survives any early dispositive motions, the parties must either settle or proceed to trial.[12] If the suit does, in fact, reach trial, the trial will result in either a defense verdict or a plaintiff verdict. In the case of a plaintiff verdict, the judge subsequently adjusts (or molds) the verdict in accordance with state law. In some states, the verdict is adjusted to account for settlement monies the plaintiff has already received. Verdicts are often appealed, and appeals can take months or years. Once all appeals have been exhausted, a judgment is entered, and the defendants found to be liable are required to pay the specified amounts.

On the far right of Figure 1.1 are trust claims. The processes that govern claim filing and payment are contained in a trust's trust distribution procedures (TDPs). To qualify for payment, a claimant must meet medical and exposure criteria that vary with the type of injury alleged. The medical criteria consist of a diagnosis and a statement of latency (the delay between first exposure to asbestos and onset of the disease). The exposure criteria address occupational exposure to asbestos and exposure to the trust's debtor's products or manufacturing facility or other conduct for which the bankrupt firm is responsible. As is discussed in Chapter Two, the trusts use criteria that are different from those used in the tort system to determine whether a claimant qualifies for compensation.[13]

Also shown in Figure 1.1 are potential linkages between the different sources of plaintiff compensation. Potential linkages include the sharing of exposure and other information relevant to the case (information linkage), the adjustment of the verdict to take account of monies received from the trusts (setoff linkage), the potential for verdict defendants to file claims with the trusts (indirect claim linkage), and trust restric-

---

[11] For more on administrative claims, see Erichson, 2005, p. 1769.

[12] More precisely, parties can settle at any time before the actual payment of the judgment. Our concern here is not with settlement behavior, per se, but with the way in which settlements are formally recognized during the trial process.

[13] An overview of trust claim-processing procedures can be found in Dixon, McGovern, and Coombe, 2010, pp. 14–22.

tions on direct claim payments (trust payment limitation linkage). We discuss each in turn.

#### Information Linkage

The sharing of trust claim forms and other information that is developed in support of trust claims presents a potential linkage between trusts and tort. Trust submissions can help defendants that remain solvent assign fault to bankrupt firms or support a solvent defendant's contention that it was not responsible for the plaintiff's injury. The information linkage is determined by whether and when claim forms and supporting exposure information that have been submitted to trusts are provided to tort defendants. Claim disclosure requirements are of little import if no claims have been filed, so requirements for when trust claims must be filed are also pertinent to the information linkage.

#### Setoff Linkage

Reductions in the verdict due to setoffs for payments received from trusts represent another linkage between trusts and tort. In tort litigation more generally, defendants often settle before trial, and, because those settlements are intended to compensate the plaintiff for the alleged harm, states often allow credit to be provided to verdict defendants for money the plaintiff has already received. Depending on state law, setoffs may be granted for trust payments in asbestos cases.[14]

#### Indirect Claim Linkage

Indirect personal injury claims provide another potential link between the tort system and trust claims. Indirect personal injury claims are claims for compensation filed with a trust by a party other than the original asbestos claimant (the direct claimant). For example, a nonsettling defendant that pays the full judgment can gain the right to pursue an indirect claim. This could occur if the plaintiff was exposed to the products of a trust's bankrupt company but, prior to the judgment, had not yet recovered money from its trust. Because the defendant covers the liability channeled to the trust (since no setoffs were granted because no money had been recovered), the verdict defendant might be able to collect the compensation that the plaintiff would have received from the trust. Note that the indirect claimant will not necessarily recover an amount corresponding to fault allocated to the bankrupt company. Instead, the amount of compensation is determined by the trust's TDP.

#### Trust Payment Limitation Linkage

Finally, restrictions in the TDPs and other documents of some trusts condition trust payments on outcomes in the tort system. For example, some trusts will not pay a

---

[14] For an extended discussion of settlement credits and contribution laws, see Eggen, 1995, p. 1701.

direct claim if another party has satisfied the trust's liability in full. This and other conditions provide feedback between the trusts and the tort case, affecting both plaintiff compensation from trust and tort combined and payments by defendants that remain solvent.

These linkages provide avenues by which the tort cases can recognize the compensation available from asbestos bankruptcy trusts and vice versa. As is apparent in the following chapters, the linkages vary considerably by state, reflecting differences in state statutes and court rules. What is more, there is often little case law addressing issues related to the various linkages. Thus, there is often some uncertainty in current linkages between trust and tort and the possibility for rapid change in the way linkages operate in practice.

## Defendant and Plaintiff Concerns About Trusts' Roles in Tort Litigation

Defendants and plaintiffs alike raise issues concerning the fairness, transparency, and proper role of asbestos trusts in the civil justice system. The problem, according to many of the defendants and defense attorneys with whom we spoke during the course of the study, is as follows. Back in the 1990s, the companies that are most frequently named as defendants in tort cases today paid less per claim than they currently do. As an increasing number of the major defendants at that time filed for reorganization, payments by the defendants that remained solvent began to increase. Trusts then came on line for the bankrupt firms, but payments per claim by defendants that remained solvent did not decline from the levels experienced during the time between the filings for reorganization and the establishment of the trusts.[15] The defendants that remained solvent believe that the reasons for this sequence of events are (1) that the bankrupt firms are not being assigned an appropriate share of fault for the alleged injury in the tort case and (2) that they are not receiving full setoffs for the payments that have been made or could potentially be made by the trusts.

Plaintiffs' attorneys with whom we spoke are concerned that the trusts are sometimes treated unfairly in the courts and that such treatment harms their clients' cases. To plaintiffs' attorneys, trusts are settling parties like any other party with which they settle. Plaintiffs are not required to settle with solvent defendants before trial, and plaintiffs' attorneys argue that the trust filing deadlines imposed in some states are inappropriate. As for defendant concerns about overpaying, plaintiffs' attorneys believe that there are adequate procedures to properly allocate liability to bankrupt firms. They also point out that defendants that remain solvent should expect to pick up that part

[15] The time between filing for reorganization and confirmation of the reorganization plan (which can include establishment of a trust) averages approximately four years (Dixon, McGovern, and Coombe, 2010, p. 29).

of the bankrupt firms' liability that is not covered by the trusts in states with joint-and-several liability.[16]

## Focus and Methods of This Monograph

This monograph examines the interaction of state tort law and civil practice rules with the trusts. Each state has its own approach for considering trust claims in the course of tort cases, and this monograph provides a snapshot of the approaches in six states. The states selected for review are California, Illinois, New York, Pennsylvania, Texas, and West Virginia. The first five states were selected because they have historically been states with a large number of asbestos filings. West Virginia was selected because of its innovative approach for dealing with the trusts. We do not examine the extent to which the practices in the selected states reflect those in other states. Thus, our findings do not necessarily capture the range of practices across the nation as a whole. We also do not examine practices in federal courts.[17]

This monograph also investigates the trusts' potential effects on total plaintiff compensation and on payments by defendants that remain solvent. It does not provide quantitative data on these effects but rather investigates whether the impacts can, in principle, be positive or negative or result in no change. Data are currently not available on trends in total plaintiff compensation or on payments by defendants that remain solvent. Although trusts publish aggregate information on the number of claims paid and total payments, the data do not allow payments to the same individual to be linked across trusts. Thus, our approach relies not on quantitative data but on characterizing the laws, rules, and court and attorney practices that together determine the trusts' effects on total plaintiff compensation and on payments by defendants that remain solvent.

Our analysis does not consider all aspects of defendant bankruptcy on plaintiff compensation and the payments by defendants that remain solvent. Specifically, we restrict our attention to reorganizations that result in a trust. We do not consider the effect of bankruptcies in which no trust is established or cases in which the firm simply dissolves without commencing a bankruptcy case.

Our analysis considers the entire litigation process from case filing to entry of a judgment against the liable parties. Although the vast majority of asbestos lawsuits settle before a final judgment is paid, the rules of civil procedure and practice establish the expectations against which settlement negotiations take place. Putting it differ-

---

16 When liability is joint and several, each of the defendants can be held liable for the entirety of the plaintiff's injury. Liability standards are further described in Chapter Two and Appendix A.

17 The majority of asbestos lawsuits are filed in state court. Between 1998 and 2000, 87 percent of new asbestos cases were filed in state court (Carroll et al., 2005, p. 61).

ently, we believe that settlement bargaining takes place in the shadow of the trial and possible judgment. Knowing the rules that govern trials, verdicts, and entry of final judgments helps provide insight into the terms under which defendants will settle, even in the absence of a trial verdict, and thus into the trusts' effect on the outcomes of interest.

To conduct our research, we engaged in a series of individual and group interviews with leading asbestos plaintiff and defense attorneys and with trust managers and counsel. Overall, we interviewed 20 defense attorneys, 11 plaintiff attorneys, and six trust managers or counsel, and some were interviewed multiple times. Each of the interviews was conducted on a confidential basis. For each selected state, we interviewed one or more lawyers from both the plaintiff and defense sides. Our protocol for the attorney interviews covered topics that included the substantive law governing liability for asbestos-related injuries, the rules for assigning fault to bankrupt firms and trusts, the discoverability and admissibility of trust claim forms and other documents submitted to trusts, the rules for setoffs, deadlines for the submission of trust claims, and the requirements for a successful indirect claim. Trust managers and counsel were asked to describe payment criteria for direct claims, compliance with requests for trust claim forms and other documents submitted to the trust, the requirements for a successful indirect trust claim, the statute of limitations on trust claims, trust provisions that affect the setoffs granted for trust payments, and provisions in trust releases limiting payment on direct claims. We also reviewed state statutes, court rules, and controlling appellate opinions. However, as noted earlier, case law often does not fully address the topics at issue.

## Organization of This Monograph

Our monograph is structured as follows. Chapter Two characterizes the liability rules and the linkages between trusts and tort in the six selected states. Chapter Three draws on the findings from Chapter Two to investigate the potential impact that the reorganizations and resulting trusts can have on total plaintiff compensation and on the amount of tort compensation paid by defendants that remain solvent. We describe a range of potential impacts by examining several hypothetical scenarios in the selected jurisdictions. Concluding observations in Chapter Four are followed by two appendixes providing more information. Appendix A provides background on how liability is allocated in the different liability regimes, and Appendix B provides more detail on the state laws and court procedures that are described in Chapter Two.

CHAPTER TWO

# Linkages Between the Trusts and Tort Cases in Six States

Because a claimant may collect money from one or more trusts and may additionally file cases in state court against solvent defendants, it is important to understand the linkages between tort and trust compensation mechanisms. Together with the underlying liability regime for asbestos-related injuries, these linkages will determine the trusts' effects on plaintiff compensation from trusts and tort combined and on the liabilities of defendants that remain solvent.

In this chapter, we first describe the liability regime in six states we have selected for analysis: New York, California, Pennsylvania, Texas, West Virginia, and Illinois. We then characterize the four linkages between trusts and tort identified in Chapter One in each of the six states:

- the information linkage: requirements on when during a tort case trust claims must be submitted and whether claim forms that have been submitted must be provided to defendants
- the setoff linkage: the extent to which verdicts are reduced to account for previous trust payments
- the indirect claim linkage: the circumstances under which a defendant will be able to recover on a claim for contribution from a 524(g) trust
- the trust payment limitation linkage: conditions under which outcomes in the tort system affect payments by the trust.

The description of each linkage is followed by an overview of the ways in which trusts are treated differently than solvent defendants in the six selected states. We conclude with an assessment of the linkages between trust and tort in our six-state sample. Appendix A provides a general overview of liability standards. Appendix B provides more detail on the specific liability standards in the six selected states, as well as on the laws, rules, and procedures described in this chapter. Appendix B also cites the statutes and court opinions that underlie the various practices.

## Liability Regime

A state's liability regime is an underlying set of rules about who can be sued for a civil harm and how fault will be apportioned between multiple tortfeasors. Key aspects of the liability regime relevant to our analysis are whether liability is joint and several, several, or some hybrid of the two (the liability standard) and whether trusts or bankrupt firms can be assigned fault in a case. In this section, we characterize both aspects of the liability regime in the six-state sample.

### Liability Standard

As shown in Table 2.1, liability for asbestos-related injuries is joint and several for both economic damages (e.g., wage loss and medical payments) and noneconomic damages (e.g., pain, suffering, and distress) in three of the states examined: Illinois, Pennsylvania, and West Virginia.[1] In these states, the plaintiff can recover the entire judgment from any one of the liable defendants. It is then up to the paying defendants to recover funds from the other parties found liable or later shown to be liable by the paying defendants. Note that, although joint-and-several states are not concerned about the apportionment of fault between joint tortfeasors as a matter of liability, juries in these states can allocate fault among the defendants to facilitate the division of payment responsibility among the liable parties. Any such apportionment does not affect

**Table 2.1**
**Liability Standards**

| State | Economic Damages | Noneconomic Damages |
|---|---|---|
| Joint-and-several-liability states | | |
| Illinois | Joint and several | Joint and several |
| Pennsylvania | Joint and several | Joint and several |
| West Virginia | Joint and several | Joint and several |
| Several-liability states | | |
| California | Joint and several | Several |
| New York | Joint and several | Several unless defendant is more than 50% at fault or reckless |
| Texas | Several unless defendant is more than 50% at fault | Several unless defendant is more than 50% at fault |

[1] Liability for asbestos injuries has recently changed in Pennsylvania and is now several, subject to some exceptions. The change does not apply to cases in which the plaintiff knew or should have known prior to June 28, 2011, that he or she was injured. The analysis in this monograph applies to Pennsylvania cases subject to this *prior* liability regime.

the overarching rule that the plaintiff can recover the entire judgment from any one defendant.

In contrast to these three states, California, New York, and Texas have several liability, at least in part, for asbestos-related injuries. *Several liability* means that a tortfeasor's liability is limited to the portion of the harm for which it is responsible, as determined in trial.

In New York, California, and Texas, the liability standards vary according to the type of damages and the degree of the defendant's relative fault. Liability remains joint and several for economic damages in California and New York. Liability for noneconomic damages is several in California in all circumstances. In New York, liability for noneconomic damages is several, except when the defendant is more than 50 percent at fault or reckless.

In Texas, liability for both economic and noneconomic damages is several, except when the defendant is more than 50 percent at fault. If a defendant is more than 50 percent at fault, the plaintiff can recover the entire judgment from that defendant (but not from other defendants that are only severally liable).[2]

These variations in the liability standard are important in many ways. To plaintiffs, a state's liability standard determines who can be sued and for what share of the total harm. In joint-and-several-liability states, a plaintiff need only sue and prove a case against one of the companies responsible for the asbestos. It seems reasonable to expect that plaintiffs would pursue those businesses with deep pockets, or the ability to pay a joint-and-several judgment. In several-liability states, however, plaintiffs face a different strategic choice about which defendants to pursue. The court will treat each defendant as a separate entity against which the claim must be proven. Thus, evidence will need to be gathered for each named defendant. Faced with the costs of this proposition, some plaintiffs might choose to name a subset of the full number of joint tortfeasors, hoping that the named defendants will be assigned a higher proportion of the overall fault than if all parties were named. This would save effort on developing evidence for all possible defendants, and potentially shift the burden and the cost to the defense to prove a case against a responsible third party (RTP).

Liability standards are important to the defendants for projecting how much a solvent defendant will have to pay and in planning trial strategy. Defendants might have an interest in attributing fault to bankrupt firms for the plaintiff's injury, depending on the liability standard. In states with several liability, identifying other joint tortfeasors will enable an individual defendant to reduce its liability because the verdict could assign it a smaller percentage of fault. In states with joint-and-several liability, doing so might enable a defendant to convince a jury that it is responsible for only a

---

[2] According to plaintiff and defense attorneys who practice in Texas, liability in Texas is several in the great majority of cases because it is rare that a defendant is found to be more than 50 percent at fault.

negligible fraction of the plaintiff's asbestos exposure and, thus, should be released from liability altogether.

### Assigning Fault to Trusts or Bankrupt Firms

Because the issue of apportioning fault is so important to the issue of overall compensation, we provide more-detailed information on whether a trust or a bankrupt firm can be named on a verdict sheet.[3] As shown in the second column of Table 2.2, bankrupt firms or trusts can be placed on the verdict sheet in all three of the several-liability states we examined. This facilitates the apportionment of fault among the parties, as is required by several-liability standards. To have a bankrupt firm or trust listed on the verdict sheet, sufficient evidence (as defined by state doctrine) must be presented during the trial. Both plaintiff and defendant can move to add parties to the verdict sheet: plaintiffs because they are presenting a primary case against such parties, and defendants because they seek to demonstrate liability or a portion thereof on the part of an RTP not originally named by the plaintiff.

**Table 2.2**
**Assigning Fault to Bankrupt Firms or Trusts**

| State | Can Bankrupt Firms or Trusts Be Placed on the Verdict Sheet? | Do Defendants Place Bankrupt Firms on the Verdict Sheet? |
|---|---|---|
| Joint-and-several-liability states | | |
| Illinois | No | — |
| Pennsylvania | No, except for 2 or 3 of the older trusts | No; even when defendants can place a trust or bankrupt firm on the verdict sheet, plaintiffs and defendants report that they rarely do so |
| West Virginia | Remains an open question | — |
| Several-liability states | | |
| California | Yes | Yes, but some defendants say that sufficient evidence to include bankrupt firms is usually lacking |
| New York | Yes | Yes, but defendants say that it is difficult to prove up a case against a bankrupt firm |
| Texas | Yes | Yes, but fewer and fewer are placed on verdict sheets since 2007 *Borg-Warner* decision |

3 The verdict sheet is submitted to the jury at the beginning of jury deliberations. It lists the parties that the jury can consider in determining liability for the plaintiff's injury. As will be discussed later, the verdict sheet can, in some jurisdictions, include parties that do not appear at trial.

The situation, however, is quite different in states with joint-and-several liability. According to attorneys with whom we spoke, defendants (and plaintiffs, for that matter) are not allowed to place trusts or bankrupt firms on the verdict sheets in Illinois. Trusts and bankrupt firms are treated no differently than parties that have entered into presuit settlements or settled after being named in an Illinois suit. These parties cannot be included on the verdict sheet either.

In Pennsylvania, a trust can be included on the verdict sheet if permitted by the documents that govern the operation of trust.[4] However, according to the attorneys and trust representatives we interviewed, such provisions appear in the documents of only two or three of the older trusts (e.g., the Manville Trust). Consequently, the vast majority of trusts cannot be included on a verdict sheet in Pennsylvania.[5] The bankrupt firms can never be added to a verdict sheet in Pennsylvania. In contrast, solvent parties that have settled can be included on the verdict sheet, although, if the plaintiff does not concede the liability of the settling party, the remaining defendants must prove up a case against the settling solvent parties.

West Virginia rules and court decisions are not clear regarding whether bankrupt firms or trusts can be on the verdict sheet. Plaintiffs' attorneys who practice in West Virginia argued that the bankruptcy channeling injunction prevents bankrupt firms from being included on the verdict sheet. In contrast, a defense attorney pointed to an example in which a judge allowed the jury to allocate fault to an "other" category that could, in principle, include bankrupt firms. According to the attorneys interviewed, cases over the past five years have settled too soon to test these theories. Settling solvent defendants are not included on the verdict sheet in West Virginia.

Even when defendants are able to place bankrupt firms on the verdict sheet, they are often reluctant or find it difficult to do so (see last column of Table 2.2). For example, some defense attorneys in Pennsylvania do not believe that it is in their clients' financial interest to name trusts, due to the way setoffs are determined for trust payments.[6] Defendants have placed bankrupt firms or trusts on the verdict sheets in California, New York, and Texas, according to attorneys with whom we spoke who practice in these states. However, our interviews indicate that trust-naming practices in these states vary across defendants. Some defense attorneys report that they seldom attempt to place bankrupt firms on the verdict sheet because evidence is usually lacking. Others indicate that they make an effort to assign fault to bankrupt firms but

[4] *Baker*, 2000.

[5] Practices may change under the modifications in Pennsylvania liability that were enacted on June 28, 2011.

[6] Pennsylvania defense attorneys are concerned that the trust will be assigned a pro rata share of the verdict but that the amount paid by the trust will be far below the pro rata share. The verdict defendant would then have to pick up the unpaid portion of the trust's pro rata share. See the "Assigning Fault to Trusts or Bankrupt Firms" section in the Pennsylvania section of Appendix B for a numerical example.

with mixed results.[7] Because this is a contentious issue, we summarize the arguments we heard from attorneys on both sides regarding the placement of bankrupt firms on verdict sheets, but we do not evaluate the merits of these arguments.

Defense attorneys indicated that it is difficult to place trusts on the verdict sheet in the three several-liability states examined. For example, the June 2007 *Borg-Warner* decision in Texas, as interpreted by the Texas asbestos multidistrict litigation judge (Mark Davidson), requires defendants to establish the proximity, frequency, and duration of exposure to the bankrupt firm's product in order to place a bankrupt firm on the verdict sheet. Trust claims, assuming that they have been filed, might be enough to establish exposure but typically will not provide the information necessary to determine the proximity, frequency, and duration of exposure.

Defense attorneys in California and New York also indicated that it is very difficult to place bankrupt firms on the verdict sheet because evidence is usually lacking: The plaintiff is often the best source of the information needed to assign fault to the bankrupt firm, but plaintiffs have an incentive to withhold cooperation.[8] The plaintiff can testify that he or she worked with or around a particular product and supply the information needed to establish exposure to the product of the bankrupt firm. However, from the defense perspective, plaintiffs are typically unwilling or unable to provide the required information. In the view of most defense attorneys, plaintiffs' attorneys control the testimony provided by the plaintiffs and coach plaintiffs not to mention the products of bankrupt firms.[9] Trust claim forms and work histories, although useful for establishing that a plaintiff was at a site, do not necessarily establish that the plaintiff was exposed to the particular asbestos-containing product in question. The result, according to defense attorneys, is that defendants are rarely successful in assigning fault to bankrupt firms.

---

[7] According to some plaintiffs' attorneys, one reason that defendants might shy away from assigning fault to bankrupt firms is that such evidence could tend to establish the defendant's own fault or be a basis for punitive damages.

[8] Defense attorneys point to examples in which a plaintiff is unwilling or unable to acknowledge exposure to a bankrupt firm's products. *Hessong* (2011, p. 66) provides one example in which plaintiff affidavits are contradicted by trust claim filings. *Kananian* (2007) provides a similar example. The distribution procedures of some trusts do little to deter such behavior. For example, the Owens Corning/Fibreboard Trust states that "failure to identify OC [Owens Corning] or Fibreboard products in the claimant's underlying tort action, or to other bankruptcy trusts, does not preclude the claimant from recovering from the PI [personal injury] Trust, provided that claimant otherwise satisfied the medical and exposure requirements of this TDP" (Section 5.7[b][3]). Although there are examples of inconsistency between plaintiff affidavits and testimony and trust claim submissions, systematic analyses have not been conducted on its prevalence.

[9] According to several defense attorneys, it is not uncommon for plaintiffs to no longer mention a once–frequently named defendant once that defendant has filed for reorganization. As an example of plaintiff coaching, defense attorneys point to a memo by Baron and Budd, a leading plaintiff firm. The memo advises their clients on how best to respond to defense attorney questions, with such instructions as "Do NOT mention product names that are not listed on your Work History Sheets. The defense attorney will jump at a chance to blame your exposure on companies that were not sued in your case" (Baron and Budd, undated).

Plaintiffs we interviewed believed that it is no more difficult for defendants to prove up a case against a bankrupt firm or a trust than it is for plaintiffs to prove up a case against a solvent defendant. They point out that evidentiary standards, such as the *Borg-Warner* standard in Texas, apply to both plaintiffs and defendants. With regard to the discovery of evidence, plaintiffs' attorneys argued that the information needed to assign fault to the bankrupt firms is available to the defense through normal discovery means. Plaintiffs are required to answer extensive interrogatories on their work histories and asbestos exposures. Defendants can use these interrogatories to formulate questions for depositions. They can assemble product identification books with pictures of the bankrupt firms' products to help refresh the plaintiff's memory during a deposition. They can locate and depose co-workers. Furthermore, according to plaintiffs' attorneys, the absence of an adversarial attorney representing a bankrupt firm makes it easier for the remaining defendants to assign fault to the bankrupt firm or its trust.

## The Information Linkage: Filing, Disclosure, and Timing of Trust Claims

A logical starting place for the examination of linkages between the trust claiming process and the tort system is in the access that defense attorneys have to documents filed with the trusts. Because trust claim submissions allege an asbestos-related harm and seek compensation, tort defendants are interested in obtaining these documents. The trust claim forms are useful to defendants for multiple reasons. The first is to complete an attorney's understanding of the sources of asbestos exposure. This might be considered an evidentiary issue. Second, trust claim forms begin a process that might lead to payments, and defense attorneys would like to account for money already received by the claimant. Overall, then, trust claim forms are a source of interest as a matter of disclosure (for evidence) and timing (for compensation). In this section, we describe the ways in which six states have managed this interest in claim forms.

### Disclosure of Trust Claim Forms

As shown in the second column of Table 2.3, plaintiffs are typically required to disclose the trust claim forms they have already submitted. In Pennsylvania, West Virginia, New York, and Texas, the disclosure requirement is part of a standard or master discovery order. In California and Illinois, the defendants must request the disclosure of the claim forms during discovery. Our interviews suggest that courts routinely grant these requests. However, although courts generally require plaintiffs to disclose trust claim forms, defense attorneys report that plaintiffs' attorneys sometimes do not comply with these orders or delay their disclosure.[10]

---

[10] For an example of controversy surrounding the timing of trust claim disclosure, see *Hessong*, 2011, p. 66.

**Table 2.3**
**Filing and Discovery Requirements for Trust Claim Forms**

| State | Are Plaintiffs Required to Disclose Trust Claims That Have Been Filed? | Is There a Requirement Regarding When Trust Claims Must Be Filed? |
|---|---|---|
| Joint-and-several-liability states | | |
| Illinois | Yes; not part of master discovery order, but judges usually grant requests for claim forms | No |
| Pennsylvania | Yes; standard discovery order in Philadelphia requires disclosure 120 days before trial | No, except in Montgomery County, where trust claims must be filed 120 days before trial |
| West Virginia | Yes; case management order requires disclosure 120 days before trial | No, but plaintiffs must investigate all potential claims 120 days before trial |
| Several-liability states | | |
| California | Yes; judges routinely grant request for claim forms | No |
| New York | Yes; required by case management order | Yes; claims must be filed 90 days before trial |
| Texas | Yes; master discovery order requires that claim forms be disclosed 60 days before trial | No, but plaintiffs are required to identify trusts from which they plan to recover |

Concerned that plaintiffs' attorneys sometimes do not disclose all trust submissions, some defense attorneys have asked trusts whether plaintiffs have filed claims, and they have requested copies of any such claim forms. Defense attorneys reported to us that trusts often do not respond to their information requests. Trust officials interviewed for this study, however, indicated that they do respond to properly executed subpoenas, as required in the trusts' governing documents. The problem, in their view, is that defense attorneys often do not go through the proper procedures to execute a subpoena.[11]

### Timing of Trust Claim Submissions

Court-ordered disclosure of filed trust claim forms is of little consequence if trust claims have not been filed. Here, we enter another contentious area: whether there is strategic behavior in the timing of trust claim submissions. Again, we report summaries of our interviews with plaintiff and defense attorneys on the topic, while not evaluating the merits of the statements.

---

[11] Although trusts often grant requests for information regarding a single claim, they have resisted the blanket requests for large numbers of claims that have been made in recent bankruptcy filings. See, e.g., *In re ACandS*, 2008.

The plaintiff and defense attorneys interviewed had differing perceptions regarding when plaintiffs actually file trust claims. Some defense attorneys reported that plaintiffs typically wait to file trust claims until after the tort case has settled or after a judgment has been entered. This opens the possibility of compensation above and beyond the amount recovered at trial. Others said that plaintiffs typically file claims against some trusts before trial but will often be eligible for compensation from other trusts.

Practices appear to vary across plaintiffs' attorneys. Some reported that they frequently delay filing until after the tort case is resolved. Others said they routinely file trust claims early in the case. Plaintiffs' attorneys identified multiple reasons to file trust claims early. First, the plaintiff might need money right away. Second, they are concerned that trust payment percentages will drop over time and that waiting to file will result in a lower recovery. Third, the statute of limitations on trust claims discourages potential claimants from waiting too long.[12]

There are also factors that militate against early filing. Plaintiffs' attorneys are concerned that defendants will attempt to use the information in the trust claim to persuade the jury that there was more exposure to the bankrupt firm's product than actually occurred. A plaintiff's attorney must also decide whether it is in his or her client's best interests to allocate scarce legal resources to develop the information needed to recover from a trust early on in a case rather than to develop the case against defendants that remain solvent. Several plaintiffs' attorneys have concluded that the benefit of distributing money to their clients sooner rather than later outweighs any potential strategic advantage of delayed trust filings and, thus, file trust claims as soon as the information required to do so becomes available. Other plaintiffs' attorneys indicated that it was their ethical obligation to their clients to delay filing if the information would assist the defendants in assigning liability to the bankrupt firms.

Regardless of the strategic choices made by attorneys, some states have addressed the issue by requiring trust claims to be filed by a certain date relative to a scheduled trial. The last column of Table 2.3 indicates whether state courts have imposed requirements on when trust claims must be filed. The attorneys with whom we spoke who practice in California and Illinois indicated that there are no filing requirements in these states. With the exception of Montgomery County (a county in suburban Philadelphia), there is no filing requirement in Pennsylvania. According to the attorneys with whom we spoke, there are no formal claim filing deadlines in Texas or West Virginia either, but plaintiffs' attorneys in these states are required to identify the trusts

---

[12] Defendants argue, however, that plaintiffs are able to satisfy the statute of limitations by filing an incomplete claim that can be later reactivated. Each trust establishes its own statute of limitations on trust claims. The statute of limitations is usually three years from diagnosis, although trusts typically will toll the claim filing requirement for three years from when the trust starts accepting claims.

from which they plan to recover.[13] Defense attorneys, however, commented that, when asked from which trusts they plan to recover, plaintiffs' attorneys in Texas will commonly state that they plan to investigate potential trust recoveries after the tort case has been resolved.

Beginning in March 2010, the court in Montgomery County required plaintiffs to file "any and all Asbestos Bankruptcy Trust claims available to him or her" 120 days before trial.[14] Like Montgomery County, New York City also has a filing deadline for asbestos cases brought there. Trust claims must be filed 90 days before trial; however, our interviews suggested that this deadline is not regularly observed. New York defense attorneys contend that plaintiffs' attorneys do not regularly comply with this filing requirement. In one plaintiffs' attorney's view, the New York filing requirement is not legally enforceable—providing support for the defense contention that plaintiffs fail to regularly comply with the filing requirement. We have not investigated whether there are filing deadlines in New York courts outside New York City.

## The Setoff Linkage: Setoffs for Trust Payments

When a verdict has been returned in favor of a plaintiff, the judge molds the verdict into an appropriate judgment to take into consideration payments made by settling parties (see discussion in Chapter One). Setoffs for payments that have already been made determine the amount owed by the verdict defendants and how much the plaintiff will collect on a final judgment.

Just as the state court rules on the timing of trust claim submissions and the placing of trusts on verdict sheets vary from state to state, so do setoff procedures. As shown in the second column of Table 2.4, setoffs for trust payments are allowed, with some exceptions, in the joint-and-several-liability states we examined. Setoffs are allowed for all pre-verdict trust payments in Illinois and West Virginia, as well as for all pre-suit settlements and settlements with solvent defendants.[15] Setoffs for trust payments are also allowed in Pennsylvania but, until recently, only when the trust or bankrupt firm is found to have contributed to the plaintiff's injury. As discussed earlier, there are only a few different trusts that can appear on the verdict sheet in Pennsylvania, and defendants typically choose not to prove up a case against those that can appear. Consequently, restricting setoffs in Pennsylvania to parties that are found liable will

---

[13] *In re Asbestos Personal Injury Litigation*, Section 22(E), 2010. Asbestos cases in West Virginia are consolidated in Kanawha County.

[14] *Thibeault*, 2010, pp. 2–3.

[15] Our discussion focuses on setoffs for pre-verdict trust payments as opposed to payments made between the verdict and when the judgment is entered. Although it appears to be the case that trust payment made in the months or years that can elapse between verdict and judgment will be treated similarly to pre-verdict trust payments, we have not systematically examined this issue.

**Table 2.4**
**Setoffs for Pre-Verdict Trust Payments**

| State | Are Setoffs Allowed for Pre-Verdict Trust Payments? | What Type of Setoff Is Allowed? |
|---|---|---|
| Joint-and-several-liability states | | |
| Illinois | Yes | Pro tanto |
| Pennsylvania | Historically only if the trust is found liable; however, a recent lower court decision allowed setoffs for payments by trusts that were not found liable | Pro tanto |
| West Virginia | Yes | Pro tanto |
| Several-liability states | | |
| California | Not for noneconomic damages except in special circumstances; yes for economic damages | Pro tanto |
| New York | Yes; reduces the total amount of the verdict that the plaintiff can recover | Greater of the total settlements received and the combined fault of the settling parties (a bankrupt firm not assigned fault does not add to the combined fault of the settling parties) |
| Texas | Only when the cap limiting total recovery to the amount of the verdict is binding | Pro tanto |

typically mean that defendants will not receive setoffs for pre-verdict trust payments. A recent opinion from the Court of Common Pleas of Philadelphia County indicates that setoff policies in Pennsylvania may be in a state of flux. In that opinion, Judge Stephen E. Levin allowed setoffs for payments by trusts that did not appear on the verdict sheet.[16] At the time of this writing, it was not clear whether other judges would follow suit, and the case is on appeal.

Although setoffs for trust payments have typically been allowed in Pennsylvania only when the bankrupt firm has been found responsible for the plaintiff's injury, the same is true for presuit settlements and settlements by solvent parties. However, settling solvent parties can be included on the verdict sheet in Pennsylvania, while most trusts cannot.[17]

When setoffs are allowed in the joint-and-several-liability states, they are pro tanto, meaning that the verdict is reduced dollar for dollar by the amount paid by the trust (see the last column of Table 2.4).[18]

---

16 *Reed*, 2010.

17 Practices might change under the modifications in Pennsylvania liability rules that were adopted on June 28, 2011.

18 The pro tanto setoff for trust payments in Pennsylvania is based on a court ruling that addressed payments by the Manville Trust (*Baker*, 2000). Its applicability to other trusts is uncertain.

The setoff provisions are more nuanced in the several-liability states. Liability for economic damages is joint and several in California, and pro tanto setoffs are allowed for the portion of trust payments than can be attributed to economic damages.[19] In contrast, setoffs are not allowed for noneconomic damages except in special circumstances. Each verdict defendant is liable for its several share of the noneconomic damages and thus, in most cases, is not entitled to a setoff for the portion of any trust settlement that is attributed to noneconomic damages.[20] The amount of previous settlements is immaterial, and payments by trusts are treated no differently than presuit settlements and settlements by solvent parties.

The situation is different in New York and Texas. Setoff rules in New York are complicated (see Appendix B), but the bottom line is that a verdict for noneconomic damages is reduced by at least the amount paid by trusts and other settling parties pre-verdict. Trusts thus contribute dollar-for-dollar to this lower bound on the setoff. Texas does not allow the plaintiff to recover more than the verdict amount. Verdict defendants are thus responsible for their allocated share of fault when liability is several unless the sum of pretrial settlements and payments by verdict defendants would exceed the verdict amount. If the sum exceeds the verdict amount, the total that can be recovered from the verdict defendants is reduced until the sum equals the verdict amount. Therefore, trust payments can reduce the amount owed by the verdict defendants, although not necessarily by the entire dollar amount of the trust award. (For a numerical example, see the section on setoffs in Texas in Appendix B.)

Our discussion of setoffs has so far addressed trust payments that have already been received by the plaintiff prior to molding the verdict. The availability of setoffs for trust claims that have been received does not mean, of course, that the verdict defendants will receive credit for payments by all trusts from which the plaintiff could potentially recover.[21] As established in Table 2.3, Texas and West Virginia require plaintiffs to identify the trusts from which they either plan to recover or could potentially recover. However, potential recoveries in Texas are not included in setoff calculations. The March 2010 case management order in West Virginia allows the court to require the plaintiff to disclose "the amount received or reasonably expected to be received"

[19] See Appendix B for a more detailed discussion of the setoff provisions in California and the methods use to allocate trust payments between economic and noneconomic damages.

[20] According to some of the attorneys interviewed, California allows setoffs for noneconomic damages in some circumstances. For example, if a distributor of asbestos products is found liable in California, it might qualify for a setoff for the payment by the trust of the reorganized defendant that supplied the distributor with the asbestos products. We have not been able to investigate this issue.

[21] Defense attorneys who practice in several of the selected states indicated that they would petition a judge to require pending trust claims to be resolved before a verdict is molded; however, doing so would still not address trust claims that had not been filed. In addition, such a petition would not address future payments from trusts that were not yet operational or make up payments that might be paid by some trusts. Makeup payments might occur, for example, if a trust increased its payment percentage and augmented payments to previously paid claimants. (The Manville Trust has made such payments.)

from trusts or any settling defendant.[22] A defense attorney interpreted this provision to either (1) allow for setoffs for the amount reasonably expected to be received or (2) require the plaintiff to pursue all trust claims before a verdict is paid. It remains to be seen how this provision of the case management order will be implemented.

## The Indirect Claim Linkage: Indirect Trust Claims

Trusts allow defendants to bring claims under certain circumstances. The provisions that govern such indirect claims are very similar or identical for many trusts. We outline the requirements for an indirect claim by referencing the procedures set out in the Owens Corning *Asbestos Personal Injury Trust Distribution Procedures*. Our discussion focuses on the language in TDPs rather than observed practice because there have been very few indirect claims. The rarity of these claims is not in itself surprising: Very few cases are tried to verdict, and even fewer result in the entry of a judgment.

The TDPs set out conditions under which an indirect claim is presumed to be valid. If a defendant cannot meet the requirements for a presumptively valid claim, the defendant can still receive payment if it meets a more general requirement. The Owens Corning Fibreboard Trust treats an indirect claim as presumptively valid if

> (a) such claim satisfied the requirements of the Bar Date for such claims established by the Bankruptcy Court . . .
>
> (b) the holder of such claims (the "Indirect Claimant") establishes to the satisfaction of the Trustees that
>
>> (i) The Indirect Claimant has paid in full the liability and obligation of the Trust to the individual claimant to whom the PI Trust would otherwise have had a liability or obligation . . .
>>
>> (ii) the Direct Claimant and the Indirect Claimant have forever and fully released the Trust from all liability to the Direct Claimant, and
>>
>> (iii) the claim is not otherwise barred by a statute of limitation or repose or by other applicable law. . . . In addition, no Indirect Claim may be liquidated and paid in an amount that exceeds what the Indirect Claimant has actually paid the related Direct Claimant.

In addition, to establish a presumptively valid claim,

---

[22] *In re Asbestos Personal Injury Litigation*, 2010.

> the Indirect Claimant's aggregate liability for the Direct Claimant's claim must also have been fixed, liquidated and paid fully by the Indirect Claimant by settlement (with an appropriate full release in favor of the PI Trust) or a Final [court] Order (as defined in the Plan) provided that such claim is valid under applicable state law.[23]

If an indirect claimant cannot meet the requirements for a presumptively valid claim, the indirect claimant may request that the trust review the claim to determine

> whether the Indirect Claimant can establish under applicable state law that the Indirect Claimant has paid all or a portion of a liability or obligation that the PI Trust had to the Direct Claimant. . . .[24]

The latter option is basically the same as showing that the indirect claimant would have a contribution claim against the bankrupt firm if it were not protected by the bankruptcy channeling injunction. Outside of situations in which some parties have declared bankruptcy, a joint tortfeasor will have a contribution claim against another party if the defendant can show that it paid all or a part of the liability of that party.[25]

Given these guidelines, indirect claims will not likely succeed when liability is several. When liability is several, a defendant is responsible for only its portion of the harm and does not cover the liability of the bankrupt firm. As an extreme example, consider a verdict in a several-liability state in which no fault was assigned to a bankrupt firm, 100 percent of the fault is assigned to solvent defendants, and the plaintiff succeeds in recovering each liable party's several share. The verdict has thus been satisfied, but it would appear that none of the verdict defendants would be able to recover from the trust because no defendant had paid the liability of the bankrupt firm.

If a verdict were satisfied in a single-satisfaction state with joint-and-several liability, the trust counsel with whom we spoke indicated that indirect claims would be successful. The indirect claimant would, of course, need to satisfy the exposure requirements for a direct claimant. In a single-satisfaction state, an injured party cannot file a court case against one set of parties for a particular loss and then file another case against a different set of parties for the same loss subsequent to the resolution of the

[23] Owens Corning Fibreboard Asbestos Personal Injury Trust, 2010, Section 5.6.

[24] Owens Corning Fibreboard Asbestos Personal Injury Trust, 2010, Section 5.6.

[25] Indirect claims can be brought, in principle, after settlement in an asbestos case, as opposed to following payment of a verdict. However, we focus on indirect claims following a verdict because there would be little reason for a defendant to cover the liability of a reorganized defendant as part of a settlement. In cases in which the plaintiff is willing to release the reorganized defendant from liability, the amount available from the trust would presumably be no more than the amount the plaintiff would require from the defendant for the release. Thus, there would be no reason for the defendant to agree to such a release.

first case.[26] Thus, once a verdict has been paid, the plaintiff has no right to any further recovery, and the defendant has, in effect, paid any liability that the trust might have to the injured party.

West Virginia has proactively addressed the availability of trust payments to defendants that have paid a verdict. Plaintiffs in West Virginia assign to the verdict defendants the right to bring trust claims, and it is the intent of the case management order that the trust treat the defendant's claim "exactly as if the claimant had submitted the claim for any and all purposes under the terms, conditions and provisions of the trust claim procedures."[27] The indirect claimant would need to satisfy only the exposure and other requirements that apply to a direct claimant.

There have been very few indirect contribution claims brought by tort defendants. The only such claims we were able to identify were those brought by Garlock Sealing Technologies in 2007 and 2008. Liability is joint and several in Maryland, and Garlock paid the judgments, after appropriate setoffs, for three asbestos personal injury cases brought in Maryland.[28] Garlock subsequently filed indirect claims with between 13 and 15 trusts for each of the cases (with substantial overlap in the trusts pursued for each claim). Garlock counsel with whom we spoke indicated that the trusts were not initially responsive to their indirect claims and that Garlock sued the trusts for response. In fact, Garlock had to ask a court to order the trustees of at least one trust to create indirect claiming procedures so that Garlock could proceed with its indirect claim. Garlock ultimately received payments in 2009 and 2010 from five or six trusts

---

[26] All the states selected for analysis in this study are single-satisfaction states. Cases that indicate that the single-satisfaction rule applies follow. For California, see *Jhaveri*, 2009 ("An injured person is entitled to only one satisfaction of judgment for a single harm, and full payment of a judgment by one tortfeasor discharges all other [sic] who may be liable for the same injury"); for Illinois, *Saichek*, 2003) (noting that Illinois "adheres to the single recovery principle [which] holds that there may not be more than one recovery of damages for a single, indivisible injury" and affirming co-defendant's motion to dismiss where plaintiff had been awarded and paid the full amount of damages by other co-defendants following entry of a default judgment in her favor); for New York, *Kotler*, 1968 (malpractice action against hospital not barred by rule that "does not permit [a] double satisfaction for single injury" because plaintiff had received only partial payment of judgment from co-defendant) and *Parchefsky*, 1935 ("the law does not permit a double satisfaction for a single injury, and for that reason we have held that satisfaction by the original wrongdoer of all damages caused by his wrong bars action against the negligent physician who aggravated the damage," quotations omitted); for Pennsylvania, *Greenleaf*, 1999 ("Under Pennsylvania law . . . 'although a plaintiff may obtain a judgment against several tort-feasors for the same harm, he or she is entitled to only one satisfaction for that harm'"); for Texas, *Lundy*, 2008 ("The single recovery, or one satisfaction rule is a rule of general acceptance that an injured party is entitled to one satisfaction for sustained injuries"); and, for West Virginia, *Pennington*, 1992 ("It is generally recognized that there can only be one recovery of damages for one wrong or injury. Double recovery of damages is not permitted; the law does not permit a double satisfaction for a single injury").

[27] *In re Asbestos Personal Injury Litigation*, 2010.

[28] The three cases were *Puller* (2002), *Snyder* (2001), and *Wilson* (2001) (all brought in the Circuit Court for Baltimore City, Md.).

for each of the tort cases.[29] According to Garlock counsel, not all the trusts that eventually paid on the indirect claims were apportioned fault in the case.

## Trust Payment Limitation Linkage: Trust Limits on Payments to Direct Claimants

Since trusts offer both direct and indirect claim payment procedures, it behooves a trustee to protect itself against paying twice on the same claim. The documents of some trusts contain language that precludes payment to direct claimants when there might be a valid indirect claim. For example, the Owens Corning Fibreboard Asbestos Personal Injury Trust requires the direct claimant to sign a release stating that the direct claimant

> represents that no judgment debtor has satisfied in full the Trust's liability with respect [to] the Injured Party's Asbestos Personal Injury Claim as the result of a judgment entered in the tort system.[30]

Releases for the U.S. Gypsum Trust and the DII Industries Trust contain almost identical clauses, and the Celotex TDPs contain language with similar effect.[31] The most likely circumstance under which such a provision would come into play is when liability is joint and several and a defendant satisfies a verdict in a single-satisfaction state. As discussed previously, the verdict defendant would likely be able to recover from the trusts. The above clause, however, would preclude recovery by the direct claimant. This type of provision has been applied in practice. One trust official with whom we spoke was aware of direct claims that had been denied when a verdict had been satisfied in single-satisfaction state with joint-and-several liability.

According to a trust official with whom we spoke, this clause would not come into play in a several-liability state. When liability is several, a party will not pay the

---

[29] Cassada, 2011. The indirect claims that were denied were denied because the direct claimant would not have been eligible for payment under the trusts' exposure criteria.

[30] Owens Corning Fibreboard Asbestos Personal Injury Trust, undated, Section 11.

[31] The Celotex trust allows trust claims when the case has been tried to verdict, although it prohibits payment once the judgment has been fully satisfied:

> "[T]he Trustees shall, except for good cause, waive their rights under single satisfaction or election of remedies laws or similar laws or [sic] that would foreclose claimants who have previously tried cases to judgment against other asbestos defendants from proceeding with claims against the Trust. . . . [T]he Trustees shall . . . not pay an amount that would result in a payment of more than the full value of such claim, injury or damage." (Celotex Trust, 2008, Section 7.15)

However, such a provision is apparently rare.

liability of another party. Thus, direct claims will be allowed in several-liability states without regard to what occurs in the tort case.

Not all trusts contain language that bars payment to the direct claimant when the trust's liability has been satisfied in full. For example, no such language appears in the release for the Armstrong World Industries Asbestos Trust.[32] A representative of one large trust said that his trust processed direct and indirect claims on separate tracks and that there is nothing in his trust procedures that would prevent both a direct and an indirect claim from being paid. Others familiar with trust operations said that such practices were the exception, not the rule.

So far, we have discussed conditions under which a direct claim will not be paid in the first place. Some trusts also allow recovery of payments made to a direct claimant when the trust is subsequently required to pay an indirect claim. A provision in several trust releases we reviewed requires that

> [t]he Claimant will hold the Trust harmless, to the extent of payment hereunder, excluding attorney's fees and costs, from any and all liability arising from subrogation, indemnity, or contribution claims, related to the OC Asbestos Personal Injury Claim released herein, from any compensation or medical payments due, or claimed to be due, under any applicable law, regulation or contact.[33]

Such a provision provides further protection against the possibility that a trust will pay twice for the same injury. We have not been able to determine how common such provisions are nor whether trusts have ever recovered payments made to direct claimants.

The discussion in this subsection indicates that some trusts have multiple tools to guard against the possibility that direct claimants will recover for damages that have been paid by another party. Indeed, some of the attorneys with whom we spoke noted that trusts jealously guard their assets and are on the lookout for circumstances in which an injured party would receive trust compensation for damages that were covered by another source.[34]

Plaintiffs' attorneys in New York said that, even though there may be no bar to obtaining recovery for their clients from some trusts once a verdict has been fully satisfied, they would not do so. They felt that bringing a trust claim in such circumstances would be ethically inappropriate because the plaintiff was compensated in full and that doing so would damage the firm's reputation.[35] There is no guarantee, however, that other plaintiffs' attorneys would feel the same way.

---

[32] Armstrong World Industries Asbestos Trust, 2010.

[33] Owens Corning Fibreboard Asbestos Personal Injury Trust, undated, Section 6.

[34] For example, some trusts require the indirect claimant to identify the direct claimant. Thus, any potential duplication of payments could quickly be identified.

[35] It is not always the case that a several-liability verdict is fully satisfied, so plaintiffs' attorneys in New York might seldom face such a situation. To fully recover, the jury would have to completely allocate fault (less any

## Extent to Which Trusts Are Treated Differently from Solvent Defendants

The attorneys with whom we spoke who played a lead role in setting up the trusts said that they strove to structure the trusts so that they would be treated the same as solvent parties in tort litigation. As evidenced by the preceding discussion, they succeeded, to some extent. For example, setoffs for trust payments are, in most cases, the same as for settlements by solvent defendants. The evidence required in the several-liability states to assign fault to the bankrupt firms is the same as for solvent defendants or in presuit settlements. Also, exposure information contained in trust claim forms is discoverable, as is exposure information developed for settlements with solvent defendants. However, trusts are treated differently from solvent defendants in a number of ways.

First, although defendants can bring solvent parties that have not been named by the plaintiff into a case, they cannot implead trusts. The several-liability states we examined address this issue by allowing trusts to be added to the verdict sheet. In contrast, trusts cannot be entered on the verdict sheet in Illinois, and most cannot be included on the verdict sheet in Pennsylvania. Uncertainty remains over whether trusts can be placed on the verdict sheet in West Virginia. Whether the inability to name trusts makes it more difficult for solvent defendants to show that they were not responsible for a plaintiff's injury needs further investigation.

Second, in at least one state, setoffs for trust payments are handled differently than setoffs for settlements by solvent defendants. In Pennsylvania, setoffs are allowed only for payments by joint tortfeasors (as opposed for all payments related to the injury). Because most bankrupt firms and trusts cannot be assigned fault, setoffs are not available for most trust payments. In contrast, settled solvent parties can be included on the verdict sheet in Pennsylvania, so the defendants will receive setoffs for payment by these parties if the jury finds them at fault. As noted earlier, a recent lower court opinion did allow setoffs for all trust payments, so practice in Pennsylvania may be changing. Another difference between the trust and settled solvent defendants in Pennsylvania is that setoffs for payments by solvent defendants are typically pro rata, while setoffs for trusts are pro tanto.

Third, verdict defendants face a lighter burden in recovering funds from some trusts post-verdict than from solvent defendants. To bring a contribution claim against a solvent co-defendant, a defendant must show that it paid more than its share of the liability and the co-defendant paid less than its share. Presumably, the co-defendant would have to be found at fault by the trier of fact or the verdict defendant would be required to show in a subsequent action that the party was indeed at fault. Trusts, in contrast, will pay an indirect claim in a single-satisfaction state with joint-and-several

fault assigned to the plaintiff) to individual defendants, and the plaintiff would have to successfully collect from each one. Research suggests that partial recovery of awards occurs in at least one-quarter of all plaintiff verdicts (Shanley and Peterson, 1987; Pace, Seabury, and Jain, 2011).

liability once the judgment has been satisfied. The verdict defendant will need to prove only the exposure requirements that the trust has established for a direct claimant, which can be far weaker than the evidence needed to prove liability against a party in a tort case.

Fourth, some courts have imposed filing deadlines for trust claims, while there are no similar requirements on when and how many solvent defendants must be pursued in a case. As discussed earlier, plaintiffs in Montgomery County, Pennsylvania, must file trust claims 120 days before trial, and New York plaintiffs must file all trust claims 90 days before trial. In some of the other states examined, there are no strict filing requirements for trust claims, but plaintiffs must notify defendants of all trust claims that may exist.

Finally, plaintiffs can still recover from trusts after a tort case has been resolved. When liability is several, there is no restriction on direct claims once all parties have settled or a judgment has been paid. When liability is joint and several, a plaintiff can still bring trust claims when all parties have settled, but usually not if a verdict has been satisfied. In contrast, once a tort case has been resolved in a single-satisfaction state, the plaintiff cannot pursue additional solvent parties.

## Summary of Linkages Between Trusts and Tort Cases

This chapter has examined the laws, court rules and procedures, and trust provisions and procedures that determine how the funds available from trusts are considered in determining tort compensation and how tort awards in turn feed back on trust payments. We have found that the linkages between the trusts and tort cases vary a great deal by state. In some states, past and potential trust payments are integrated into tort cases; in other states, these linkages are incomplete. The linkages we examined address the filing and disclosure of trust claims, setoffs, indirect claims, and trust limits on payments to direct claimants. We discuss each in turn.

### Information Linkage

Courts in the six states examined generally require the disclosure of claim forms for trust claims that have been filed. However, such a requirement is of little consequence if plaintiffs are able to file trust claims after the tort case has been resolved. Courts in New York City and in Montgomery County, Pennsylvania, require all trust claims to be filed before trial, but there is no such requirement in the other states examined. Delayed filing could deprive defendants of important information regarding exposure to the products of the bankrupt firms. The result may be that not all the relevant exposure information is considered in the resolution of the tort case. Instead, exposure information not considered in the tort case might be used to recover from trusts outside the tort case. One would not expect complete exposure information to be developed in any tort case and would expect plaintiffs to focus their efforts on the defendants they have named in the case. But, absent trusts, the compensation process is complete once the tort case is resolved. When trusts are present, plaintiffs can potentially use information not considered in the tort case to obtain compensation from the trusts after the tort case has been resolved.

### Setoff Linkage

Four of the states examined (Illinois, New York, Texas, and West Virginia) allow setoffs for all pre-verdict trust payments; Pennsylvania and California do not. Defendants in California do not receive setoffs for that portion of a trust payment that the court attributes to noneconomic damages. However, the same is true for noneconomic damage settlements by solvent parties. In Pennsylvania, setoffs have typically been allowed only when the trust has been assigned fault. The same is true for settlements by solvent parties, but, in contrast to solvent parties, trusts typically cannot be assigned fault in Pennsylvania. However, Pennsylvania law regarding setoffs for trust payments may be changing.

### Indirect Trust Claim Linkage

The indirect claim process appears fairly straightforward in single-satisfaction states with joint-and-several liability. Once the verdict has been satisfied, the verdict defendant will be able to recover from the trust as long as it satisfies the exposure and other requirements that apply to the direct claimant. The hitch is that the defendant often needs the plaintiff's cooperation to develop the required information. Whether such cooperation will be forthcoming is uncertain.

Indirect claims will not be available to defendants when liability is several. This will typically not be an issue between plaintiffs and defendants, although one can imagine circumstances under which defendants could argue that they should have access to indirect claims. Recall the example in which a California verdict was fully satisfied by the severally liable defendants. The defendants might argue that they, rather than the plaintiff, should benefit from trust payments. Several attorneys familiar with trust operations emphasized that trusts have not developed guidelines for whether they would pay indirect claims in many different types of circumstances because they have received few, if any, indirect claims. Standards would presumably be rapidly established with the advent of more indirect claim submissions.

### Trust Payment Limitation Linkage

Provisions at some trusts prohibit payments to direct claimants when the trust's liability has been satisfied by another party and require direct claimants to indemnify the trust for future indirect claims. Such provisions provide feedback between outcomes in the tort system and the trust, preventing a trust from paying more than once on the same injury and reducing the likelihood that a plaintiff will receive more than the full value of injury. Although some trusts have such provisions, others do not. At trusts that do not, it is possible that trusts can pay more than once on the same claim. However, based on our interviews, it appears that most trusts are on the lookout for circumstances in which an injured party would receive trust compensation for damages that were covered by another source. Further investigation is needed to determine the fraction of trusts with clauses that restrict payment when the trust's liability has been satisfied by another party and that provide indemnification against indirect claims.

## Conclusion

This chapter has provided a descriptive overview of variation in procedures concerning asbestos claims in tort and trust across the six selected states. Our interest is in clarifying the situations in which the tort system takes cognizance of the existence, operation, and contributions of the asbestos personal injury trusts. These trusts were established to assume the asbestos liabilities of bankrupt firms. Our goal is to understand how the assumption of these liabilities has interacted with the liabilities of solvent defendants in the tort system.

The foregoing discussion presents a varied picture. Among the several areas in which the tort system could interface with the trusts, states have adopted different rules and procedures. Whether these variations are sound policy is beyond our ability to judge at this point. Data on the effect of these differing procedures are currently unavailable.

However, these different procedures likely do produce an effect on the overall level of compensation available and actually paid to asbestos claimants. Similarly, the rules and procedures likely have an effect on the ultimate amount paid by solvent defendants in the tort system. In the next chapter, we use what we have learned about the variations in procedure to hypothesize the effect on plaintiff compensation and solvent-defendant payments.

CHAPTER THREE

# Potential Effects That Trusts Can Have on Total Plaintiff Compensation and Payments by Defendants That Remain Solvent

Rules and litigant practices regarding the disclosure of trust claims, the assignment of liability to bankrupt firms, setoffs for trust payments, and indirect trust claims determine the trusts' effect on total plaintiff compensation and on the liability of defendants that remain solvent. In this chapter, we hypothesize how trusts' replacement of once-solvent defendants can affect the total compensation received by plaintiffs and payments by defendants that remain solvent in the six states examined.

## Range of Potential Effects

The actual impact that bankruptcies and the creation of asbestos personal injury trusts can have on plaintiff compensation and payments by defendants that remain solvent is an empirical question; however, the direct answer to that question is impeded by a lack of data. Settlements, which constitute the lion's share of asbestos resolutions, are kept confidential. Although data on settlements would reveal much about the trusts' effect on overall compensation, such information is not readily available at this time.

Yet, it is still possible to investigate the range of possible effects given (1) the rules and procedures from Chapter Two concerning setoffs and indirect recoveries and (2) a few basic assumptions about asbestos litigation both pre- and post-reorganization. To better understand the possible impact that the reorganizations and subsequent establishment of the trusts could have on total plaintiff compensation and payments by defendants that remain solvent, we consider the following thought experiment. Assume first that all the potential defendants in an asbestos personal injury case are solvent and that the jury returns a verdict in favor of the plaintiff, assigning no fault to the plaintiff and allocating liability to the defendants in accordance with state liability rules. We will refer to this situation as the *pre-reorganization scenario.* Now consider the same plaintiff facing the same jury in the same state, but with some of the defendants reorganized and trusts up and running in their place. We will refer to this situation as the *post-reorganization scenario.* Further assume that the jury verdict is the same in both situations.[1] We split defendants into two groups: defendants that are reorganized and defendants that remain solvent. Defendants that are reorganized are solvent in the pre-reorganization scenario and reorganized with a trust paying claims in their place in the post-reorganization scenario. Defendants that remain solvent are solvent in both the pre- and post-reorganization scenarios.

In this section, we examine the potential difference in the payments by these two defendant groups pre- and post-reorganization. The change in aggregate payments by defendants that are reorganized is the amount paid by the trusts set up in the post-reorganization scenario less the amount paid in the pre-reorganization scenario by firms that will later file for reorganization. The change in payments by defendants that remain solvent is the amount paid in the post-reorganization scenario less the amount paid in the pre-reorganization scenario.[2] The change in plaintiff compensation from trust and tort combined is the total plaintiff compensation in the post-reorganization scenario less the total compensation in the pre-reorganization scenario.

Table 3.1 runs through various cases for payments by the two sets of defendants and for total plaintiff compensation. In all cases, the combined payments by the defendants that are reorganized declines by x dollars. The low payment percentage at most trusts makes these plausible scenarios. In case 1, payments by defendants that remain solvent do not change. Such an outcome might occur in states with several liability when the defendants that remain solvent are able to prove up the same case post-reorganization against the bankrupt firms. In this case, the total plaintiff compensation falls. The plaintiff bears the difference between the liability assigned to the defendants that are reorganized and the amount the trusts are actually able to pay.

In case 2, payments by defendants that remain solvent increase, but by less than the decline in payments by defendants that are reorganized. Such a scenario might occur if defendants that remain solvent in a several-liability state are not successful in proving up a case against some of the bankrupt firms and the jury increases the fault assigned to the defendants that remain solvent. Here, the plaintiff still bears some of the loss from the shortfall in the payments by the defendants that are reorganized, but some of the loss is also borne by defendants that remain solvent.

In case 3, the increase in payments by defendants that remain solvent matches the decline by defendants that are reorganized. Such an outcome might occur if liability is joint and several and defendants that remain solvent receive pro tanto setoffs for all payments made by the trusts pre-verdict and are assigned the right to recover from

---

[1] We do not consider the transition period between the time a firm files for reorganization and when a trust is paying claims in its place. We thus focus on the longer-run impact that the replacement of solvent defendants by trusts can have.

[2] It might be the case that a solvent defendant is not named and makes no payments in the pre-reorganization scenario but makes payments in the post-reorganization scenario. Similarly, it could be that a firm that is reorganized makes no payment in the pre-reorganization scenario but its trust makes payments in the post-reorganization scenario.

**Table 3.1**
**Different Cases for the Change in Plaintiff Compensation Due to Trusts**

| Case | Change in Combined Payments by Defendants That Are Reorganized | Change in Combined Payments by Defendants That Remain Solvent | Change in Total Plaintiff Compensation[a] |
|---|---|---|---|
| 1 | –x | 0 | – |
| 2 | –x | >0 and <x | – |
| 3 | –x | x | 0 |
| 4 | –x | >x | + |

NOTE: The change is the amount paid (received) in the post-reorganization scenario less the amount paid (received) in the pre-reorganization scenario.

[a] – = the change is negative. 0 = there is no change. + = the change is positive.

trusts post-verdict.[3] In this case, defendants that remain solvent in effect pick up the shortfall in the trust payments due to the payment percentage. The plaintiff receives full compensation for the harm, but defendants that remain solvent pay more than they would have prior to the bankruptcies.

In case 4, the combined payments by defendants that remain solvent increase more than the decline in payments by defendants that are reorganized, causing an increase in total plaintiff compensation. In a several-liability state, such an outcome might occur if defendants that remain solvent are unable to prove up a case against the bankrupt firms but the plaintiff is still able to recover from the trusts. For example, the jury in a several-liability state might increase the share of liability assigned to defendants that remain solvent, and the plaintiff is still able to recover from the trusts after termination of the tort case.

It is possible that the plaintiff could receive more in total from trusts in the post-reorganization scenario than from defendants that are reorganized in the pre-reorganization scenario. (The entries in the second column of Table 3.1 would be positive rather than negative.) The requirements for recovering from trusts differ from those for recovering from defendants in a tort case. Post-reorganization, a plaintiff might be successful in recovering from the trusts of defendants that would not have been found liable in the tort case pre-reorganization. The recoveries from additional trusts could hypothetically offset the drop in payments by trusts of parties that would have been found liable in the pre-reorganization scenario. In addition, there is a great deal of disagreement about the extent to which the value a trust assigns to a claim reflects the amount the reorganized defendant paid pre-reorganization. If the value assigned by the trust is sufficiently high, the amount paid by the trust might be higher

3 In this chapter, we do not consider the period between when a verdict is reached and when a judgment is entered. Due to the appeal process, this period can extend months or years.

than the amount paid by the defendants that are reorganized pre-reorganization, even after application of the payment percentage.[4]

Although it is, in principle, possible for a plaintiff to receive more from all trusts in the post-reorganization scenario than received from all defendants that are reorganized in the pre-reorganization scenario, we think that this is an unlikely scenario. We thus do not consider such a possibility in this monograph, although further work is warranted on the comparison of trust payments with payments by a reorganized defendant pre-reorganization.

These cases illustrate the range of impacts that could, in principle, occur. We now draw on the findings in Chapter Two to investigate potential outcomes in the six study states. Because the analysis is more straightforward for joint and several, we start with the states with joint-and-several liability. We then turn to the states with several-liability schemes.

## Effects in States with Joint-and-Several Liability

To assist in understanding the trusts' potential effects on the total plaintiff compensation and payments by defendants that remain solvent in joint-and-several-liability states, consider the following example. The jury awards the plaintiff $4 million in total damages. Because liability is joint and several for economic and noneconomic damages, there is no need to break the $4 million award down into economic and noneconomic damages. Further assume that, in the pre-reorganization scenario, there are four solvent parties (R1, R2, S1, and S2). Now consider the same plaintiff and the same jury verdict, but, after R1 and R2 have been reorganized, trusts are paying claims in their place, and the payment percentage for each trust is set at 25 percent. Also assume that both trusts have set the liquidated value for the type of injury suffered by the plaintiff at $1 million. Both trusts thus will pay $0.25 million (25 percent of $1 million). Assume also that one trust pays prior to the verdict.

Following the analysis in Chapter Two, we assume that a trust will pay an indirect claim when liability is joint and several, a judgment has been satisfied, and the indirect claimant can meet the exposure and other requirements that would have been required of the direct claimant. The trust will pay an indirect claim under these circumstances because all the states we have selected are single-satisfaction states and because, once a judgment has been satisfied, the verdict defendants have, in effect, covered the liability of the bankrupt firms. We also assume that a trust will not pay twice for the same injury. Although there might be exceptions, the provisions in the documents of many trusts limit the possibility that a trust will pay both an indirect and direct claim on the

4 Some of the defense attorneys and analysts with whom we spoke believe that this is indeed the case for some trusts.

same injury (see Chapter Two). Consequently, we assume that, if a trust approves an indirect claim after already paying a direct claim, the trust will recover the payment made to the direct claimant.

### West Virginia

The bankruptcies and the subsequent creation of the trusts should not, in principle, affect the total plaintiff compensation in West Virginia. In the pre-reorganization scenario, the plaintiff could recover the jury award from any one of the liable defendants, which could then recover from the other liable parties. Pro tanto setoffs for pre-verdict trust payments mean that, in the post-reorganization scenario, the plaintiff can recover the jury award less the pre-verdict trust payments from any one of the defendants that remain solvent. Once a West Virginia verdict has been satisfied, the plaintiff must assign the right to any future trust recoveries to the verdict defendants. The plaintiff can thus make no further recoveries from the trusts post-verdict, with the result that total plaintiff compensation in West Virginia would be the same in the pre- and post-reorganization scenarios. The defendants that remain solvent would end up paying more post-reorganization because of joint-and-several liability.

Such an outcome is illustrated in Table 3.2. In the pre-reorganization scenario, S1 settles for $1 million, and the remaining three defendants allocate the verdict among themselves after receiving a $1 million setoff, so that each ends up paying $1 million. In the post-reorganization scenario, the trust set up for R1 pays $0.25 million prior to the verdict and S1 settles for $1 million. Because liability is joint and several, the remaining solvent defendant (S2) is responsible for the amount necessary to satisfy the $4 million verdict ($2.75 million). The plaintiff assigns the right to recover from R2's trust to S2. Post-verdict, R2 pays $0.25 million to S2 (reflected by the $0.25 million entry for R2 and the –$0.25 million entry for S2 in the penultimate column), and the total amount received by the plaintiff remains at $4 million.

As can be seen in Table 3.2, the combined outlays by defendants that remain solvent increase from $2.0 million in the pre-reorganization scenario to $3.5 million in the post-reorganization scenario. The defendants that remain solvent first cover the reduction in trust payments due to the payment percentage. The obligations of defendants that remain solvent would further increase if their indirect claim against R2 were unsuccessful. In contrast, the amount received by the plaintiff would remain unchanged if the indirect claim were unsuccessful.

Plaintiffs in West Virginia must make "a good faith investigation of all potential [trust] claims" 120 days before trial. In terms of the ultimate payment that he or she can expect to receive from the trusts and solvent defendants, the plaintiff will receive the same amount regardless of whether he or she complies with this requirement. The plaintiff will receive $4 million as long as at least one solvent defendant is found liable. It is possible that, once the exposures to the products or practices of all bankrupt firms

**Table 3.2**
**Example of No Change in Total Plaintiff Compensation in West Virginia**

| | Pre-Reorganization Scenario | | Post-Reorganization Scenario | | | |
|---|---|---|---|---|---|---|
| **Defendant** | **Found at Fault by the Jury?** | **Payments ($ millions)** | **Found at Fault by the Jury?** | **Pre-Verdict Payments ($ millions)** | **Post-Verdict Payments ($ millions)** | **Total Payments ($ millions)** |
| Defendants that are reorganized | | | | | | |
| R1 | Yes | 1.0 | No | 0.25 | 0 | 0.25 |
| R2 | Yes | 1.0 | No | 0 | 0.25 | 0.25 |
| Total | | 2.0 | | 0.25 | 0.25 | 0.5 |
| Defendants that remain solvent | | | | | | |
| S1 | No (settles) | 1.0 | No (settles) | 1.0 | 0 | 1.0 |
| S2 | Yes | 1.0 | Yes | 2.75 | −0.25 | 2.5 |
| Total | | 2.0 | | 3.75 | −0.25 | 3.5 |
| Plaintiff compensation | | 4.0 | | 4.0 | 0 | 4.0 |

are accounted for, the jury could find that no remaining solvent defendant made a significant contribution to the injury, but that seems like an unlikely outcome.

Failure of the plaintiffs to investigate all potential claims has two downsides from the point of the view of the solvent defendants. Although the probability seems low that the resulting information might enable a solvent defendant to show that it did not make a significant contribution to the injury, the potential for such an outcome remains. The defendants with whose representatives we spoke said that they would like the ability to use all exposure information to assess whether they are responsible for the injury. Also, the absence of full investigation might mean that the defendants are not able to bring successful indirect claims, and some trust money will be left on the table. If S2's indirect claim against the trust for R2 is unsuccessful in the example provided, then the combined trust payments drop by $0.25 million, the payment by S2 increases by a like amount, and the amount received by the plaintiff remains unchanged.

Issues regarding the development of exposure information arise for defendants even in the absence of defendants that are reorganized and their trusts. An individual defendant would, in principle, like to split liability among as many other defendants as possible and would benefit from the plaintiff's investigation of all exposures. However, defendants are often reluctant to pull other solvent parties into a case, fearing that these parties will, in turn, pull them into future cases. Defendants have no such concern with the trusts.

### Illinois

The situation in Illinois is similar in many ways to that in West Virginia. Liability is joint and several, and defendants receive setoffs for all pre-verdict trust payments. However, in contrast to plaintiffs in West Virginia, Illinois plaintiffs are not required to investigate all trust claims before trial, and there is no requirement that plaintiffs assign direct claims to the verdict defendants once a judgment has been satisfied.

The absence of a requirement to assign trust claim to defendants once a judgment has been satisfied will not affect total plaintiff compensation or payments to defendants that remain solvent. Under our assumptions, the trust will pay an indirect claim arising out of an Illinois tort case if the judgment has been satisfied. Assigning trust claims to verdict defendants might be a more straightforward way to ensure that the verdict defendants are able to benefit from trust resources and that the plaintiff cannot recover money from a trust after a verdict has been satisfied, but the same outcome will be accomplished via indirect claims.

As in West Virginia, information on the exposure to products and practices of bankrupt firms can allow a solvent defendant to make a case that it was not responsible for an Illinois plaintiff's injury and to provide the information needed to file indirect claims. Plaintiffs argue that it is up to the defendant to develop evidence of the exposures the plaintiff chooses not to investigate. Defendants respond that the plaintiffs' attorneys influence which products and practices their clients remember. If the information on exposures to the products and practices of bankrupt firms does not come out, then overall plaintiff compensation in Illinois will likely not be affected, but the ability of defendants that remain solvent to take advantage of the resources available from the trusts will be diminished. If defendants that remain solvent are unsuccessful in collecting on an indirect claim, they will end up covering the entire amount paid by the firms that are reorganized in the pre-reorganization scenario rather than just the difference between what the reorganized firm would have paid in the pre-reorganization scenario and the amount available from the trust.

### Pennsylvania

Whereas verdict defendants in West Virginia and Illinois receive pro tanto setoffs for all pre-verdict trust payments, verdict defendants in Pennsylvania might not receive setoffs for some pre-verdict trust payments.[5]

Setoffs in Pennsylvania have historically been allowed for pre-verdict settlements only when the settling party is found liable.[6] With just a few exceptions for the oldest

---

5 Our analysis applies to cases in which the plaintiff knew or should have known prior to June 28, 2011, that he or she was injured.

6 As discussed in Chapter Two, a Pennsylvania trial court recently allowed setoffs for all trust payments, but it is not known whether this decision will be followed by other judges. The opinion is currently on appeal. It is also worth noting that setoffs might not be allowed for settlements by solvent parties. At issue is not whether the payment is made by a trust or a solvent party but whether the trust or solvent party is found liable.

trusts (such as the Manville Trust), trusts and bankrupt firms cannot be found liable in Pennsylvania. And, as reported in Chapter Two, even if a trust can be found liable, plaintiff and defense attorneys in Pennsylvania report that defendants do not attempt to prove up a case against it. Because liability is joint and several but defendants might not receive setoffs for pre-verdict trust payments, a plaintiff in the post-reorganization scenario might be able to recover more through the judgment than the amount awarded by the jury. However, subsequent indirect claims by defendants that remain solvent can reduce the total plaintiff compensation in Pennsylvania back to the level observed in the pre-reorganization scenario.

The example used for West Virginia is modified to illustrate a case in which defendants do not receive setoffs for pre-verdict trust payments. As shown in Table 3.3, all the parties are assigned fault in the pre-reorganization scenario. S1 settles as before, but settling solvent parties can be on the verdict sheet and found liable by the jury.[7] Thus, a setoff is available for the payment by S1.

Unlike in West Virginia and Illinois, the Pennsylvania S2 receives no setoff for the pre-verdict payments by R1's trust in the post-reorganization scenario because R1 cannot be found liable. S2 is then liable for the entire amount less the $1 million settlement received from S1. As a consequence, the plaintiff receives $4.25 million in compensation up through the verdict (see third column from the right in Table 3.3). After satisfaction of the judgment, S2 brings indirect claims against R1 and R2. Both indi-

**Table 3.3**
**Example of No Change in Total Plaintiff Compensation in Pennsylvania**

| | Pre-Reorganization Scenario | | Post-Reorganization Scenario | | | |
|---|---|---|---|---|---|---|
| **Defendant** | **Found at Fault by the Jury?** | **Payments ($ millions)** | **Found at Fault by the Jury?** | **Pre-Verdict Payments ($ millions)** | **Post-Verdict Payments ($ millions)** | **Total Payments ($ millions)** |
| Defendants that are reorganized | | | | | | |
| R1 | Yes | 1.0 | No | 0.25 | 0 | 0.25 |
| R2 | Yes | 1.0 | No | 0 | 0.25 | 0.25 |
| Total | | 2.0 | | 0.25 | 0.25 | 0.5 |
| Defendants that remain solvent | | | | | | |
| S1 | Yes | 1.0 | Yes | 1.0 | 0 | 1.0 |
| S2 | Yes | 1.0 | Yes | 3.0 | −0.50 | 2.5 |
| Total | | 2.0 | | 4.0 | −0.50 | 3.5 |
| Plaintiff compensation | | 4.0 | | 4.25 | −0.25 | 4.0 |

7 S1 can be assigned fault if S2 is able to prove up S1's liability or if the plaintiff concedes S1's liability.

rect claims will be paid because S2 has satisfied the judgment in a single-satisfaction state with joint-and-several liability. R2 has previously paid a direct claim and will recover the $0.25 million paid to the direct clamant. The result is that total plaintiff compensation returns to $4.0 million, and payments by the solvent defendants total $3.5 million. Thus, even though the defendants that remain solvent did not receive a setoff for all pre-verdict trust payments, our assumptions on trust practices pertaining to indirect claims cause total plaintiff compensation and payments by defendants that remain solvent to remain the same as in the West Virginia and Illinois examples. Pursuit of indirect claims will require the expenditure of defendant time and money, costs that defendants might not be willing to bear. Failure to collect on an indirect claim because the transaction cost is too high would keep plaintiff compensation above the $4 million level.

As discussed in Chapter Two, we have not been able to determine how widespread trust-release language is that allows the trust to recover from a previously paid direct claimant when an indirect claim is paid. If a trust does not recover from the direct claimant, the trust will pay twice for the same injury, and total plaintiff compensation can be greater in the post-reorganization scenario than in the pre-reorganization scenario.

## Effects in States with Several Liability

To illustrate the potential effects of the trusts in states with several liability, we modify the example used for the joint-and-several-liability states. We now assume that, both before and after reorganization, the jury returns a $4 million verdict for noneconomic damages. We focus on noneconomic damages because liability for noneconomic damages can be several in each of the three several-liability states selected but is joint and several for economic damages in two of the three states. We also assume in the pre-reorganization scenario that the jury assigns each of the four defendants 25 percent of the fault. As before, we assume that the liquidated value set by the trusts for the type of injury suffered by the plaintiff is $1 million and that the payment percentage is 25 percent.

In our analysis of the effects of trusts in several-liability states, we assume that indirect claims will not be successful. When liability is several, the verdict defendant pays only its share of the award and does not cover the liability of the trust. Plaintiffs, however, will be able to bring direct claims post-verdict.

### California

Replacing defendants that are reorganized with asbestos bankruptcy trusts could reduce plaintiff compensation for noneconomic damages in California. Plaintiffs would recover less if the defendants that are reorganized are assigned the same liability shares in pre- and post-reorganization scenarios and (as we have assumed) a trust's payment is less than its assigned liability. The plaintiff would then bear the burden of the reduction in the trust payments due to the payment percentage, and the payments by defendants that remain solvent would remain unchanged.

Such an outcome is illustrated in Table 3.4. The jury awards $4 million for noneconomic damages in the pre-reorganization scenario, and the plaintiff is able to recover $1.0 million from each of the defendants. The defendants that remain solvent are successful in proving up the case in the post-reorganization scenario against the bankrupt firms. Post-reorganization, the plaintiff collects $1.0 million each from S1 and S2 but collects only $0.25 million from each trust. In this example, one trust pays pre-verdict, and the plaintiff successfully recovers from the other trust post-verdict. The plaintiff in the post-reorganization scenario recovers only $2.5 million, while the amount paid by defendants that remain solvent remains unchanged at $2.0 million.

Situations can also arise in which a plaintiff recovers more in noneconomic damages in the post-reorganization scenario than he or she would recover in the pre-reorganization scenario. Consider the example in Table 3.5. The bankrupt firms are not added to the verdict sheet, and the jury allocates 100 percent of the liability to S1 and S2 in the post-reorganization scenario. Post-reorganization, the plaintiff receives the full $4 million award for noneconomic damages from defendants that remain solvent. Because there is no setoff in California for pre-verdict payments for noneconomic damages, there is no setoff for the pre-verdict payment by R1's trust. As shown in the

**Table 3.4**
**Example of a Decrease in Total Plaintiff Compensation for Noneconomic Damages in California**

| | Pre-Reorganization Scenario | | Post-Reorganization Scenario | | | |
|---|---|---|---|---|---|---|
| Defendant | Percentage of Fault Assigned | Payments ($ millions) | Percentage of Fault Assigned | Pre-Verdict Payments ($ millions) | Post-Verdict Payments ($ millions) | Total Payments ($ millions) |
| Defendants that are reorganized | | | | | | |
| R1 | 25 | 1.0 | 25 | 0.25 | 0 | 0.25 |
| R2 | 25 | 1.0 | 25 | 0 | 0.25 | 0.25 |
| Total | | 2.0 | | 0.25 | 0.25 | 0.5 |
| Defendants that remain solvent | | | | | | |
| S1 | 25 | 1.0 | 25 | 1.0 | 0 | 1.0 |
| S2 | 25 | 1.0 | 25 | 1.0 | 0 | 1.0 |
| Total | | 2.0 | | 2.0 | 0 | 2.0 |
| Plaintiff compensation | | 4.0 | | 2.25 | 0.25 | 2.5 |

**Table 3.5**
**Example of an Increase in Total Plaintiff Compensation for Noneconomic Damages in California**

| | Pre-Reorganization Scenario | | Post-Reorganization Scenario | | | |
|---|---|---|---|---|---|---|
| Defendant | Percentage of Fault Assigned | Payments ($ millions) | Percentage of Fault Assigned | Pre-Verdict Payments ($ millions) | Post-Verdict Payments ($ millions) | Total Payments ($ millions) |
| Defendants that are reorganized | | | | | | |
| R1 | 25 | 1.0 | 0 | 0.25 | 0 | 0.25 |
| R2 | 25 | 1.0 | 0 | 0 | 0.25 | 0.25 |
| Total | | 2.0 | | 0.25 | 0.25 | 0.5 |
| Defendants that remain solvent | | | | | | |
| S1 | 25 | 1.0 | 50 | 2.0 | 0 | 2.0 |
| S2 | 25 | 1.0 | 50 | 2.0 | 0 | 2.0 |
| Total | | 2.0 | | 4.0 | 0 | 4.0 |
| Plaintiff compensation | | 4.0 | | 4.25 | 0.25 | 4.5 |

bottom row of Table 3.5, total pre-verdict plaintiff compensation thus increases to $4.25 million. In addition, payments by defendants that remain solvent increase from $2.0 million to $4.0 million.

Subsequent to the verdict, the plaintiff will be able to bring a direct claim against R2's trust. Total plaintiff compensation will increase to $4.5 million as a result.

More work is needed to determine how often defendants that remain solvent in California are unable to prove up liability against defendants that are reorganized. If defendants that remain solvent are not able to prove up liability against bankrupt firms, they might pick up the liability of parties that would have been found liable in the pre-reorganization scenario. This outcome occurs because there will be no setoffs for pre-verdict trust payments for noneconomic damages in the post-reorganization scenario and because indirect claims are not available.

The increase in plaintiff compensation in Table 3.5 is not because trust payments are treated differently from settlements by solvent parties. To illustrate, replace R1 with a solvent party that, in the post-reorganization scenario, enters into a presuit settlement. There is no setoff for this presuit settlement, and, if S1 were not successful in assigning fault to R1 in the post-reorganization scenario, plaintiff compensation would increase. What is driving this increase in plaintiff compensation when trusts are involved is the inability of defendants that remain solvent to assign fault to the defendants that are reorganized.

### New York

Unlike in California, pre-verdict trust payments in New York cannot cause total plaintiff compensation to be greater in the post-reorganization scenario than in the pre-reorganization scenario. Verdict defendants in New York courts receive a setoff that is the greater of the aggregate amount received by the plaintiff and the aggregate share of fault assigned to the settling parties multiplied by the verdict amount. Thus, setoffs for pre-verdict trust payments in New York are at least as large as the amount received from the trusts. Consider the example in Table 3.6. The defendants that remain solvent in this example are unable to prove up a case against R1 and R2 in the post-reorganization scenario, and S1 and S2 are each found 50 percent at fault. S1 and S2 receive a setoff that is the greater of the aggregate settlement amount ($0.25 million) and the aggregate fault assigned to the settling parties (0 percent). S1 and S2 thus split the remaining $3.75 million, and the plaintiff receives $4 million.

Plaintiffs in New York City are required to file all trust claims before trial; however, our interviews suggest that this requirement might not be regularly observed. If the plaintiff files after resolution of the tort case, nothing will stop the trusts from paying the claims, and plaintiff compensation will increase. As shown in the last two columns of Table 3.6, the post-verdict trust claim will cause total plaintiff compensation to increase to $4.25 million. Thus, although setoff rules in New York prevent the plaintiff from recovering more than the verdict amount up through the verdict, plaintiff compensation could increase due to post-verdict trust payments. New York plain-

**Table 3.6**
**Example of an Increase in Total Plaintiff Compensation for Noneconomic Damages in New York**

| | Pre-Reorganization Scenario | | Post-Reorganization Scenario | | | |
|---|---|---|---|---|---|---|
| **Defendant** | **Percentage of Fault Assigned** | **Payments ($ millions)** | **Percentage of Fault Assigned** | **Pre-Verdict Payments ($ millions)** | **Post-Verdict Payments ($ millions)** | **Total Payments ($ millions)** |
| Defendants that are reorganized | | | | | | |
| R1 | 25 | 1.0 | 0 | 0.25 | 0 | 0.25 |
| R2 | 25 | 1.0 | 0 | 0 | 0.25 | 0.25 |
| Total | | 2.0 | | 0.25 | 0.25 | 0.5 |
| Defendants that remain solvent | | | | | | |
| S1 | 25 | 1.0 | 50 | 1.875 | 0 | 1.875 |
| S2 | 25 | 1.0 | 50 | 1.875 | 0 | 1.875 |
| Total | | 2.0 | | 3.75 | 0 | 3.75 |
| Plaintiff compensation | | 4.0 | | 4.0 | 0.25 | 4.25 |

tiffs' attorneys with whom we spoke said that they would not file trust claims when a verdict has been fully satisfied. If they hold to this position, then the plaintiff would not be able to recover more post- than pre-reorganization.

As in California, the replacement of solvent defendants by trusts could also lead to a reduction in total plaintiff compensation in New York. In Table 3.7, defendants that remain solvent are successful in allocating 25-percent fault to each of the bankrupt firms, and the trust corresponding to R1 pays \$0.25 million pre-verdict. The setoff is then the greater of \$0.25 million and 25 percent of the verdict (\$1.0 million). The plaintiff can then recover up to \$3.0 million from S1 and S2. However, because S1 and S2 are only severally liable, the maximum that the plaintiff can recover from each one is \$1.0 million, and the plaintiff receives \$2.25 million up through the verdict.[8] Post-verdict recovery from the trust established for R2 would increase the total plaintiff compensation to \$2.5 million, but compensation would remain substantially below the \$4 million the plaintiff receives in the pre-reorganization scenario.

### Texas

In Texas, defendants are liable only for their allocated share of fault, subject to the proviso that the total recovery is not greater than the verdict. Thus, excluding the possibility of post-verdict trust recoveries, Texas plaintiffs cannot recover more than the verdict award. Table 3.8 provides a case in which plaintiff compensation up through the verdict remains at \$4.0 million in the post-reorganization scenario. The defendants that remain solvent are unsuccessful in assigning fault to R1 and R2 in the post-reorganization scenario. Each is allocated 50-percent fault post-reorganization and is liable for up to \$2.0 million. If S1 and S2 each paid \$2.0 million, however, the pre-verdict trust payment would cause total plaintiff compensation up through verdict to exceed \$4.0 million. The liability of S1 and S2 are thus reduced to \$1.875 million each. S1 and S2 have, in effect, received a setoff for R1's pre-verdict trust payment.

Even though plaintiff compensation up through the verdict remains at \$4.0 million, it can increase once post-verdict trust payments are considered. When R2's trust pays the plaintiff post-verdict, total plaintiff compensation increases to \$4.25 million, and payments by the remaining solvent defendants stay at \$3.75 million. In such a situation, the defendants that remain solvent would have, in effect, covered the reduction in trust payment due to the payment percentage for the trust making payment pre-verdict and the entire liability of the bankrupt firm corresponding to the trust that made payment post-verdict.

As in California and New York, total plaintiff compensation might fall from what it would be in the pre-reorganization scenario if defendants that remain solvent are

---

[8] If one of the remaining defendants is found reckless, that defendant would be jointly and severally liable, and the plaintiff could recover the entire \$3.0 million from that party. Even considering post-verdict trust recoveries, however, the plaintiff would still recover less than the full verdict in the post-reorganization scenario.

**Table 3.7**
**Example of a Decrease in Total Plaintiff Compensation for Noneconomic Damages in New York**

| | Pre-Reorganization Scenario | | Post-Reorganization Scenario | | | |
|---|---|---|---|---|---|---|
| **Defendant** | **Percentage of Fault Assigned** | **Payments ($ millions)** | **Percentage of Fault Assigned** | **Pre-Verdict Payments ($ millions)** | **Post-Verdict Payments ($ millions)** | **Total Payments ($ millions)** |
| Defendants that are reorganized | | | | | | |
| R1 | 25 | 1.0 | 25 | 0.25 | 0 | 0.25 |
| R2 | 25 | 1.0 | 25 | 0 | 0.25 | 0.25 |
| Total | | 2.0 | | 0.25 | 0.25 | 0.5 |
| Defendants that remain solvent | | | | | | |
| S1 | 25 | 1.0 | 25 | 1.0 | 0 | 1.0 |
| S2 | 25 | 1.0 | 25 | 1.0 | 0 | 1.0 |
| Total | | 2.0 | | 2.0 | 0 | 2.0 |
| Plaintiff compensation | | 4.0 | | 2.25 | 0.25 | 2.5 |

successful in assigning fault to the bankrupt firm. In Table 3.9, R1 and R2 are each assigned 25 percent of the fault, as are S1 and S2. Total plaintiff compensation, including the post-verdict trust recovery by the plaintiff, decreases to $2.5 million.

## Synthesis of Findings on the Potential Effects of Trusts

In this chapter, we have developed a series of examples that illustrate the trusts' potential effects on total plaintiff compensation and payments by defendants that remain solvent. We have found that the potential effects vary considerably by state, reflecting the differences in liability regimes and in court rules and procedures. Some states have rules that take into account past or possible future trust payments. Others seem to treat trust payment as sui generis, outside the purview of the courts. This can allow plaintiffs to recover more from tort and trust combined than they would have recovered had none of the defendants filed for reorganization, ceteris paribus.

### Potential Effects on Plaintiff Compensation and Defendant Payments

Table 3.10 collects the findings in this chapter on the trusts' potential impact on total plaintiff compensation and payments by defendants that remain solvent. As shown in the second column of the table, one should expect no change in total plaintiff compensation in each of the three joint-and-several-liability states examined. Setoffs for all pre-verdict trust payments and the requirement that plaintiffs assign defendants the right

**Table 3.8**
**Example of an Increase in Total Plaintiff Compensation in Texas**

| | Pre-Reorganization Scenario | | Post-Reorganization Scenario | | | |
|---|---|---|---|---|---|---|
| Defendant | Percentage of Fault Assigned | Payments ($ millions) | Percentage of Fault Assigned | Pre-Verdict Payments ($ millions) | Post-Verdict Payments ($ millions) | Total Payments ($ millions) |
| Defendants that are reorganized | | | | | | |
| R1 | 25 | 1.0 | 0 | 0.25 | 0 | 0.25 |
| R2 | 25 | 1.0 | 0 | 0 | 0.25 | 0.25 |
| Total | | 2.0 | | 0.25 | 0.25 | 0.5 |
| Defendants that remain solvent | | | | | | |
| S1 | 25 | 1.0 | 50 | 1.875 | 0 | 1.875 |
| S2 | 25 | 1.0 | 50 | 1.875 | 0 | 1.875 |
| Total | | 2.0 | | 3.75 | 0 | 3.75 |
| Plaintiff compensation | | 4.0 | | 4.0 | 0.25 | 4.25 |

to post-verdict trust claims underlie the result in West Virginia. Plaintiffs in Illinois are not required to assign trust claims to verdict defendants when a judgment is satisfied, but verdict defendants will be able to bring indirect trust claims. If a plaintiff in Illinois attempts to file trust claims once a judgment has been satisfied, either the claim will be denied (some trust releases contain such a provision) or the trust will pay an indirect claim and recover any prior direct-claim payment. Setoffs have typically not been allowed for pre-verdict trust payments in Pennsylvania, but the payment of indirect claims when a judgment is satisfied and the trusts' ability to recover prior direct-claim payments when an indirect claim is paid will keep total plaintiff compensation the same in the pre- and post-reorganization scenarios. Although Pennsylvania's multistep process for recovering pre-verdict trust payments when setoffs are not granted is circuitous, it produces the same outcome for total plaintiff compensation as in Illinois and West Virginia.

As shown in the bottom part of Table 3.10, the examples we have developed indicate that outlays by defendants that remain solvent will increase in states with joint-and-several liability. Outlays by defendants that remain solvent will increase by at least the difference between what the defendants that are reorganized paid pre-reorganization and the amount paid by the trusts. But the increases will be greater if a trust does not pay either a direct or an indirect claim for the injury. In the end, the increase does not depend on whether it is the plaintiff or the solvent defendant that brings the trust claim, just on whether a trust claim is brought.

**Table 3.9**
**Example of a Decrease of Total Plaintiff Compensation in Texas**

| | Pre-Reorganization Scenario | | Post-Reorganization Scenario | | | |
|---|---|---|---|---|---|---|
| Defendant | Percentage of Fault Assigned | Payments ($ millions) | Percentage of Fault Assigned | Pre-Verdict Payments ($ millions) | Post-Verdict Payments ($ millions) | Total Payments ($ millions) |
| Defendants that are reorganized | | | | | | |
| R1 | 25 | 1.0 | 25 | 0.25 | 0 | 0.25 |
| R2 | 25 | 1.0 | 25 | 0 | 0.25 | 0.25 |
| Total | | 2.0 | | 0.25 | 0.25 | 0.5 |
| Defendants that remain solvent | | | | | | |
| S1 | 25 | 1.0 | 25 | 1.0 | 0 | 1.0 |
| S2 | 25 | 1.0 | 25 | 1.0 | 0 | 1.0 |
| Total | | 2.0 | | 2.0 | 0 | 2.0 |
| Plaintiff compensation | | 4.0 | | 2.25 | 0.25 | 2.5 |

**Table 3.10**
**Summary of Potential Effects of the Trusts in the Six States Examined**

| | Liability Standard | |
|---|---|---|
| Potential Impact of Trusts | Joint and Several | Several |
| Total plaintiff compensation | | |
| Decrease | | x |
| No change | x | x |
| Increase | | x |
| Payments by defendants that remain solvent | | |
| Decrease | | |
| No change | | x |
| Increase | x | x |

Outcomes can be very different in the three several-liability states examined.[9] In all three states, the replacement of once-solvent defendants by trusts can cause total plaintiff compensation to decrease or increase. Although we have not developed any numerical examples, total plaintiff compensation could also remain unchanged if the factors that cause an increase in total plaintiff compensation balance out those that cause a decrease. Thus, as shown in the last column of Table 3.10, a decrease, no change, or increase in total plaintiff compensation is possible in the three several-liability states examined. In contrast to the outcomes for the joint-and-several-liability states, we have found that payments by defendants that remain solvent can either remain unchanged or increase in the several-liability states (see bottom part of Table 3.10).

The potential increase in total plaintiff compensation in several-liability states is not because setoffs for trusts are different from those for settling solvent defendants. Indeed, setoffs, when they exist in the several-liability states, are the same for the two sources of compensation. The factors that enable an increase when trusts are involved are (1) plaintiffs' ability to recover trust payments after the tort case has been terminated, (2) solvent defendants' inability to bring indirect claims when liability is several, and (3) the fact that direct claims will be allowed regardless of what transpires in the tort system. The result is that payments by defendants that remain solvent are not adjusted for pre-verdict payments when trust payments do not generate setoffs. Likewise, payments by defendants that remain solvent are not adjusted for postjudgment trust payments.

### Importance of Evidence on Exposure to the Products and Practices of Bankrupt Firms

How trusts affect total plaintiff compensation and payments by defendants that remain solvent depends in large part on whether information is developed on exposure to the products and practices of bankrupt firms and on the timing of trust claims. Figure 3.1 illustrates what is at stake for plaintiffs and solvent defendants. In the pre-reorganization scenario (panel 1), defendants that remain solvent pay A and the defendants that will be reorganized pay B + C. C represents the amount that the trusts will pay post-reorganization, and B represents the amount that the trusts will not cover (the split between B and C reflects the trusts' payment percentages).[10] The amount received by the plaintiff (A + B + C) is the sum of the amounts received from defendants that remain solvent and from defendants that will be reorganized. Cross-hatching denotes amounts that are paid through or received from the tort system.

---

[9] Liability is joint and several for economic damages and can be joint and several for noneconomic damages in some of the several-liability states examined. We restrict our attention here to situations in which liability is several.

[10] Thus, for example, if the defendants that file for reorganization pay \$1 million pre-reorganization and the payment percentage is 25 percent, B would be \$0.75 million and C would be \$0.25 million.

**Figure 3.1**
**Range of Outcomes Possible in the Joint-and-Several-Liability States Compared with Those in the Several-Liability States**

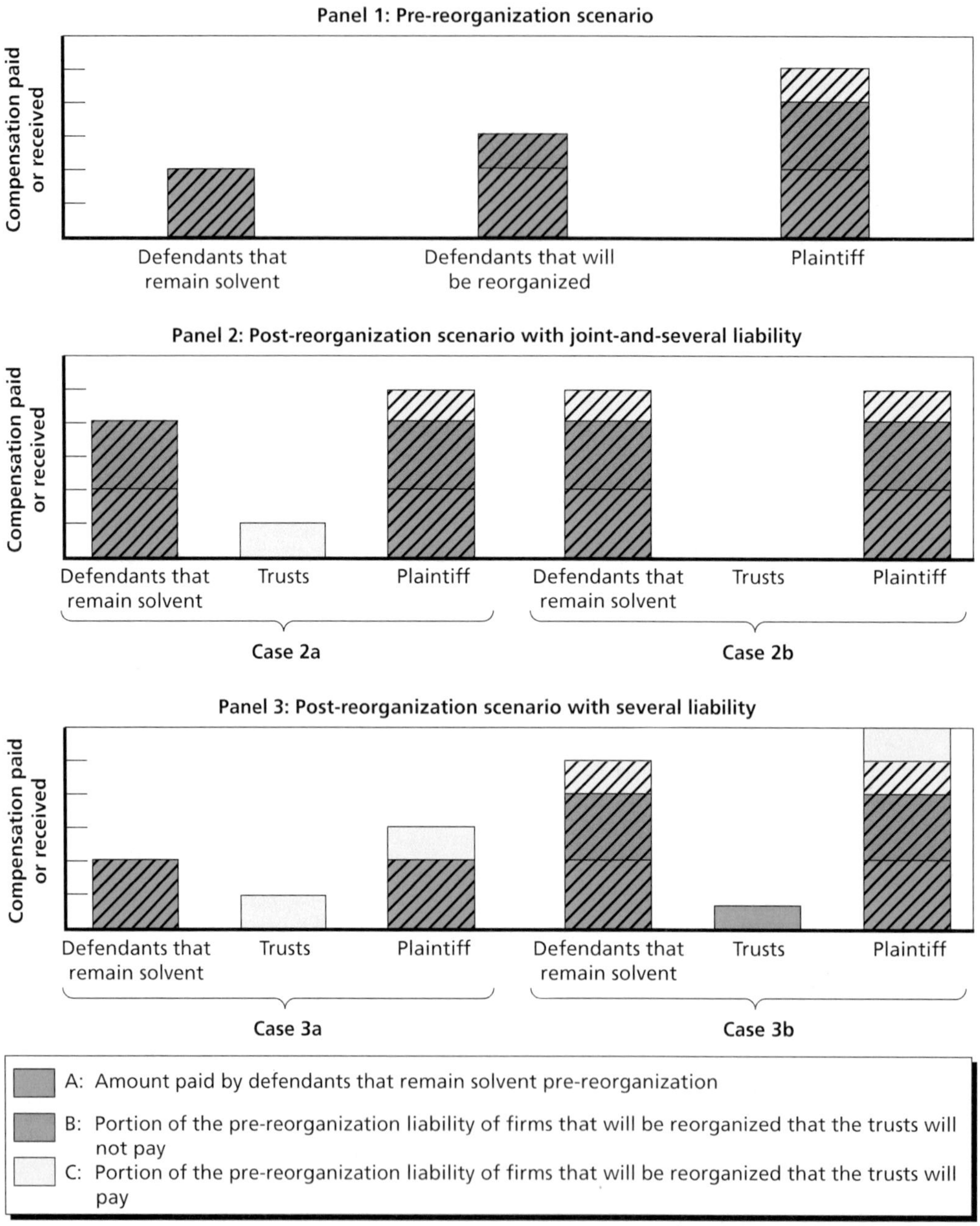


NOTE: Cross-hatched areas denote the amount paid through the tort system.

RAND *MG1104-3.1*

Panel 2 in Figure 3.1 presents the range of outcomes that could result in states with joint-and-several liability. If all potential claims are brought against the trusts, the trusts pay C, and defendants that remain solvent pay A + B (see case 2a in panel 2). Defendants that remain solvent cover the difference between what defendants that are reorganized pay pre-reorganization (B + C) and what the trusts pay post-reorganization (C). Plaintiff compensation remains at A + B + C. Such an increase is consistent with the intent of joint-and-several liability—a plaintiff can recover from any one defendant, and the defendant is responsible for other defendants' shares that cannot be collected. In case 2b, evidence for trust claims is not developed, and no direct or indirect trust claims are brought. Total plaintiff compensation remains at A + B + C, but defendants that remain solvent now pay A + B + C. In this case, the defendants that remain solvent are not able to take advantage of the compensation available from the trusts.

The increase in the amount paid by defendants that remain solvent between the pre- and post-reorganization scenarios depends on the extent to which exposures to the products or practices of bankrupt firms are uncovered and trust claims brought by either the direct or indirect claimant. As can be seen from comparing cases 2a and 2b, what is at stake for defendants that remain solvent in joint-and-several-liability states is thus C, the amount of potential trust payments. Plaintiffs have nothing at stake in terms of total plaintiff compensation because single-satisfaction rules and joint-and-several liability should fix the value of total plaintiff compensation at A + B + C.

The stakes for plaintiffs and defendants that remain solvent regarding the development of evidence on exposure to bankrupt firms are greater in the several-liability states (see Figure 3.1, panel 3). When information on all exposures to the products and practices of bankrupt firms is available, the outcomes in case 3a could result. Defendants that remain solvent pay A, the trusts pay C, and plaintiff compensation falls to A + C. If no information on exposures to the products and practices of bankrupt firms is available and all trust claims are brought after payment of the judgment, then the outcomes in case 3b could result. In this case, the jury assigns 100 percent of the fault to the parties that remain solvent post-reorganization, and defendants that remain solvent pay A + B + C. The plaintiffs would still be able to recover from the trusts post-verdict, increasing total plaintiff compensation to A + B + C + C. The plaintiff has been able to recover once in the tort system and then receive extra compensation from the trusts. Such an outcome is not consistent with a several-liability doctrine that holds a defendant responsible only for its share of the fault. However, it does avoid the drop in total plaintiff compensation that occurs in case 3a.

By comparing cases 3a and 3b, one can see that the amount at stake for defendants that remain solvent is B + C in the several-liability states, larger than the C in the joint-and-several-liability states. Plaintiffs have nothing at stake in terms of total compensation when liability is joint and several. In several-liability states, B + C is now at stake.

If plaintiffs are looking to maximize total plaintiff compensation, an effective strategy in several-liability states is to pursue only claims against the named defendants, delaying the investigation of trust claims until the tort case is concluded. Doing so can allow the plaintiff to recover more than in the pre-reorganization scenario if the plaintiff is able to increase the percentage of fault that the jury allocates to defendants that remain solvent in the post-reorganization scenario compared to what the jury would have allocated to them in the pre-reorganization scenario. Submission of trust claims after termination of the tort case is desirable for the plaintiff because doing so can avoid disclosure of information that could aid in assigning fault to the bankrupt firms. It is also desirable because, although there are no setoffs for trust payments received after the tort case has terminated, there are setoffs to varying degrees for pre-verdict trust payments in some of the jurisdictions examined. Of course, the plaintiff might decide to file trust claims early in the case anyway if a high value is placed on receiving some compensation early on rather than waiting for settlements from solvent defendants or the payment of a judgment.

Defendants that remain solvent are not prohibited from developing evidence on the products and practices of bankrupt firms during the course of an asbestos suit. To take advantage of the resources available from trusts in joint-and-several-liability states, it is not necessary for defendants to develop information that, in principle, would be sufficient to hold trusts or bankrupt firms liable. Rather, all that is required is the information needed to bring a successful trust claim, which is typically less comprehensive than that required to establish liability. However, it still may be difficult for defendants to develop the information needed for all trust submissions without the cooperation of the plaintiff.

Among the joint-and-several-liability states examined, West Virginia has proactively addressed issues regarding the investigation of trust claims. As discussed in Chapter Two, it requires the plaintiff or the plaintiff's counsel to complete a "good faith investigation of all potential claims against asbestos trusts" 120 days before trial. This requirement was adopted in March 2010, and what is required in a good-faith investigation will become clear only over time.

Evidence that is sufficient to bring a trust claim can help defendants in several-liability states if plaintiffs file trust claims pre-verdict and there are setoffs for pre-verdict trust payments (as in New York). Even if 100 percent of the fault is assigned to defendants that remain solvent, as long as all trust claims are filed pre-verdict and setoffs are available, total plaintiff compensation would be the same in the pre-reorganization and post-reorganization scenarios. Defendants that remain solvent would cover the difference between what reorganized defendants paid in the pre-reorganization scenario and what the trusts pay in the post-reorganization scenario (B in Figure 3.1). Although such an outcome is clearly preferable for defendants that remain solvent to one in which they receive no setoffs, they are still paying more than in the pre-reorganization scenario. To keep payments at pre-reorganization levels in several-liability states, defendants that remain solvent must assemble evidence that is sufficient to assign fault to bankrupt firms. Doing so typically requires more-comprehensive information than needed to bring trust claims, and defendants argue that they cannot develop such information without the cooperation of plaintiffs. Of course, such cooperation might mean that the plaintiff receives less than in the pre-reorganization scenario.

The case management order in New York City addresses the timing of trust claims in a several-liability setting. It requires plaintiffs to file all trust claims before trial. Compliance with the requirement would prevent an increase in total plaintiff compensation in the types of examples examined in this chapter. However, it would not necessarily prevent an increase in payments by defendants that remain solvent unless the filings enable defendants that remain solvent to assign fault to defendants that are reorganized. There are no trust filing requirements in California and Texas, and defense attorneys in New York City with whom we spoke do not believe that the filing order is routinely complied with in New York City.

CHAPTER FOUR

# Conclusion

Aggregate payments by asbestos bankruptcy trusts are substantial and, given the sizable assets of existing and expected future trusts, likely to stay that way for years to come. The reservoir of potential asbestos personal injury claims is large and also likely to stay that way for many years. Thus, both plaintiffs and defendants that remain solvent have a great deal at stake with regard to how trusts enter into the determination of tort awards.

The objective of our analyses has been to better understand the extent to which trust payments or the potential for trust payments is considered in the determination of tort awards and to identify trusts' potential impacts on total plaintiff compensation and payments by defendants that remain solvent.

## Implications of the Findings

In order to achieve the study objectives, we examined the linkages between the trusts and tort cases. We considered the litigation and trust recovery process from presuit settlements to the potential recovery on indirect claims following satisfaction of a judgment. We found first that there is a great deal of variation across states in the laws and court procedures that determine the extent to which trust compensation is considered in tort cases. Liability standards vary by state, as do practices regarding setoffs and assigning fault to bankrupt firms. There is also considerable variation across the states examined regarding when during a tort case trust claims must be investigated or filed.

We found that, in many cases, pre-verdict trust payments are considered in the determination of the tort judgment. However, in some cases, they are not. In California, for example, defendants do not receive setoffs for noneconomic damage payments by trusts.[1] Defendants in Pennsylvania also do not receive setoffs for payments by most trusts, although Pennsylvania law on this issue may be changing.

[1] Although pre-verdict trust payments are treated the same as pre-verdict settlements by solvent parties, it still remains the case that, when no fault is assigned to a trust in California, the remaining defendants will not receive any offset for pre-verdict trust payments.

The indirect claim linkage works very differently when liability is joint and several than when liability is several. When liability is several, indirect claims are not available. When liability is joint and several, indirect claims allow solvent defendants to recover from trusts once the judgment has been satisfied. Indirect claims can also allow solvent defendants to, in effect, recover pre-verdict direct claim payments that did not result in a setoff.

As for the information linkage, in most of the states examined, plaintiffs are not required to file trust claims before the resolution of a tort case. The absence of filing deadlines can prevent all compensation available from the trusts from being considered in the tort case. When trust claims are not filed prior to trial, defendants will not receive setoffs for trust payments and might not have the information they need to assign fault to bankrupt firms at trial or to pursue indirect trust claims postjudgment.

We also examined the potential effects that reorganization can have on total plaintiff compensation and on the payments by defendants that remain solvent. We found that potential outcomes in states with joint-and-several liability are fundamentally different from those in states with several liability. In states with joint-and-several liability, our analysis indicates, the trusts should not affect total plaintiff compensation. In contrast, the trusts can cause total plaintiff compensation in states with several liability to decrease, remain unchanged, or increase. In the extreme, a plaintiff can receive full compensation in the tort system and then receive additional compensation from the trusts. Such an outcome is not consistent with the doctrine in several-liability states that holds defendants responsible for only their share of the fault. Although the additional trust payments benefit current plaintiffs, they can disadvantage future plaintiffs in several-liability states. The additional trust payments deplete trust assets, reducing the amount available for future payments. If, for example, no solvent party is found liable in a future case, the plaintiff's only source of compensation will be the trusts. Additional trust payments to current plaintiffs could thus translate into lower total compensation for the future plaintiff.

Turning to payment by defendants that remain solvent, we found that payments by defendants that remain solvent will increase in states with joint-and-several liability. We have identified circumstances under which the payments by defendants that remain solvent increase by the amount of the bankrupt firms' pre-reorganization liability that is not covered by the trusts. Such an increase would be consistent with the intent of joint-and-several liability. We have also identified circumstances under which the increase would be greater, indicating that the defendants that remain solvent in joint-and-several-liability states are not benefitting from the resources available from the trusts.

Turning to the several-liability states, we have found that payments by defendants that remain solvent can either remain unchanged or increase. Increases are inconsistent with the several-liability principle that a defendant should be responsible for only its share of the fault. However, such increase can mean that total plaintiff compensation does not fall from the pre-reorganization scenario.

The difference in outcomes by liability regime is driven by defendants' ability to file indirect claims once a judgment has been satisfied in joint-and-several-liability states. When liability is joint and several, indirect claims provide a mechanism to adjust payments made by the remaining defendants and compensation received by the plaintiff. Remaining defendants can recover from the trusts via indirect claims, and trust payments to plaintiffs can be recovered by the trusts if it is determined that the defendant is eligible for an indirect claim (this might happen if there was no offset for a pre-verdict trust payment). In contrast, when liability is several, the plaintiff can receive trust payments after the tort case is resolved, and the absence of indirect claims means that there is no way to adjust payments by defendants that remain solvent. Likewise, the lack of indirect claims means that there is no way to recoup pre-verdict trust payments that did not result in setoffs.

Our findings underscore the importance of information on exposure to the products and practices of the bankrupt firms. Information on exposure to the products and practices of bankrupt firms does not affect total plaintiff compensation in joint-and-several-liability states (as long as at least one solvent defendant is found liable). However, it does affect payments by defendants that remain solvent: Less information can mean fewer trust claims and higher payments by defendants that remain solvent. When liability is several, an absence of exposure information can lead to an increase in plaintiff compensation if the remaining defendants are no longer able to assign fault to the bankrupt firms post-reorganization. An absence of such information can also mean that payments by the remaining defendants are higher than they would be otherwise.

There is a great deal of dispute between plaintiff and defense attorneys over who is responsible for developing evidence on the products and practices of bankrupt firms. Plaintiffs' attorneys argue that defense attorneys can use discovery tools to uncover exposure information. Defense attorneys respond that plaintiffs' attorneys can influence the exposures plaintiffs recall during the court case and that, without plaintiff cooperation, they will not succeed in assembling the information needed to recover from the trusts. We have not examined the dynamics of the discovery process. We note, however, that the stakes regarding the development of this information are greater for both plaintiffs and the defendants that remain solvent in states with several liability than in states with joint-and-several liability. This could create different incentives to investigate, or avoid investigating, exposures to the products and practices of bankrupt firms in joint-and-several-liability states from those to investigate or avoid investigating similar exposures in several-liability states.

Some states have addressed the disputes between plaintiffs and defendants regarding the investigation and filing of trust claims. Plaintiffs in New York City are required to file all trust claims at least 90 days before trial, and West Virginia plaintiffs are required to complete a good-faith investigation of all trust claims no later than

120 days before trial. These rules have the potential to affect total plaintiff compensation and payments by defendants that remain solvent. The New York rule could cause the replacement of once-solvent defendants by asbestos trusts to increase total plaintiff compensation and payments by defendants that remain solvent less than would have been the case without such a requirement. The West Virginia rule could cause payments to the remaining solvent defendant to increase less than they would otherwise.

## Limitations and Next Steps

Although our analysis has identified the trusts' potential effects on total plaintiff compensation and payments by defendants that remain solvent, it has not determined what actually occurs in practice. Data over time on the expenditures by defendants that remain solvent are needed to better understand both the direction and magnitude of the effects. Such data, however, are currently unavailable. Data on trust outlays and on how trust payments compare to what defendants are reorganized paid pre-reorganization would also help to pin down the effects. Information from plaintiffs on total compensation for cases that resolved pre- and post-reorganization in different jurisdictions would be a tremendous value; however, that information has historically not been available.

Although we have examined laws and court procedures in states that have had substantial asbestos case loads, our analysis has addressed only six states. The situations in these states might not capture the range of situations that exist in other states. Examination of laws and rules in other states is warranted.

We have assumed in our analysis that the amount paid by a trust is less than what the party that filed for reorganization would have paid in tort prior to filing for reorganization. Although this appears to be a plausible assumption for most trusts, further work is needed to confirm its validity and, if it does not hold, to evaluate the consequences for total plaintiff compensation and payments by defendants that remain solvent.

Finally, our analysis has not evaluated whether the current system for compensating asbestos victims is functioning well or poorly. Rather, it has attempted to describe the linkages between the trusts and tort cases and the potential implications of these linkages. Such an assessment would require a set of goals for the performance of the asbestos compensation system. Goals pertaining to transaction costs, the intent of the liability standard, time to disposition, and single satisfaction for a wrong might be considered. We leave it to future work to assess the performance of the multisource system in place today for compensating asbestos victims and to suggest reforms that will improve outcomes.

APPENDIX A

# Background on Liability Standards

Knowing a state's liability standard is important for determining an asbestos claimant's potential compensation at the end of a trial. The state liability standard establishes who can be sued and the requirement for finding liability and helps to calculate how much a defendant might have to pay if it loses at trial. Three methods of assigning liability to joint tortfeasors are used in the United States:

- joint-and-several liability
- modified joint-and-several liability
- several liability.

Depending on the jurisdiction in which a suit is brought, each of the defendants could be liable for the entirety of the worker's injury, or each could be responsible only for its share of the harm. The state's choice of liability standard is ultimately a question of policy. Different liability rules serve different policy interests. We discuss each in turn.

*Joint-and-several liability* means that the plaintiff may seek full recovery from any of the co-defendant joint tortfeasors. If Acme and Apex are jointly and severally liable and the amount of damages is $10 million, Amy may seek $10 million from either Acme or Apex (though she is not entitled to $10 million from each). Joint-and-several liability ensures that an injured plaintiff has the legal right to seek full recovery from any of the responsible parties that contributed to the harm, regardless of the tortfeasor's relative level of fault.

Joint-and-several-liability rules relieve some burdens on the plaintiff because the plaintiff can recover the full amount of the injury even if one or more responsible tortfeasors cannot pay their share of the damages. If, for example, Acme went bankrupt, Amy could still seek the full $10 million from Apex (even though Apex did not exclusively cause Amy's illness).

*Several liability* means that a tortfeasor's liability is limited to the portion of the harm for which it is responsible, as determined in a trial. Several liability links a defendant's potential judgment for a joint harm to its individual share of the injury. No defendant is responsible for paying more than its proportionate liability. For example, if Acme is found 30 percent responsible and Apex is found 70 percent responsible,

Acme can be held to no more than $3 million out of the total $10 million harm. Generally speaking, plaintiffs in several-liability states must succeed in convincing the jury to assign 100 percent of the fault to solvent parties in order to recover the full value of the injury.[1] Moreover, a plaintiff must absorb any losses caused by a bankrupt defendant's inability to pay a judgment. The plaintiff in a several-liability state may not recover the bankrupt defendant's share from any other party. If, for example, Apex went bankrupt, Amy could recover, at most, $3 million from Acme (and Amy suffers the $7 million loss herself).

*Modified joint-and-several liability* is a miscellaneous category of liability rules that blends elements of joint-and-several liability and several liability. For example, some states impose joint liability on a tortfeasor only if it behaves recklessly toward the plaintiff or if the defendant's share of liability exceeds some preestablished threshold (the other parties in the case could still only be severally liable). These reforms were passed to dampen the effect of joint-and-several liability for tortfeasors that contributed a minority share of the joint harm.

Consider the following. Acme and Apex are joint tortfeasors. Their actions cause a $10 million harm to Amy. Before Amy files suit, Apex declares bankruptcy. Amy sues Acme in a modified joint-and-several-liability state with a 50-percent threshold. A 50-percent threshold means that the liability standard is several liability unless the defendant is found more than 50 percent responsible. Beyond the 50-percent mark, the defendant is jointly and severally liable. At trial, Acme is found 30 percent liable; Apex 70 percent. Amy can recover, at most, $3 million from Acme. Alternatively, if Acme had been the bankrupt company, ceteris paribus, Amy could have recovered the full $10 million from Apex because Apex's apportioned liability share was above the 50-percent threshold.

---

[1] A jury might assign some share of the liability to an "other" category. The plaintiff would not be able to recover this portion of the award.

APPENDIX B

# Liability Rules and Court Procedures Relevant to Asbestos Bankruptcy Trusts in Six States

This appendix details the liability rules and court procedures relevant to trusts in the six states selected for detailed analysis. The findings are based on interviews with plaintiff and defense attorneys who practice in the selected states, as well as review of state statutes, court rules, and controlling appellate opinions.

## Areas Covered in State Overviews

For each state, practices are summarized in the following areas:

- *Liability standard.* Describes how responsibility for satisfying judgments is allocated among co-defendants.
- *Assigning fault to trusts or bankrupt firms.* Describes whether fault can be assigned to bankrupt firms and the criteria that must be satisfied to assign fault to bankrupt firms.
- *Timing of trust claims.* Reports whether requirements exist for when trust claims must be filed during a tort case. Also describes the typical filing practices according to the attorneys with whom we spoke.
- *Discoverability of trust claims.* Indicates whether discovery or other procedural rules require plaintiffs to disclose claim forms that have been submitted to trusts. In states without established requirements, indicates whether judges typically grant defendants' requests for trust claims. Also reports perceptions of both plaintiff and defense attorneys regarding whether plaintiffs' attorneys comply with disclosure requirements and orders.
- *Admissibility of trust claims.* Discusses whether information submitted in support of trust claims is typically admissible as evidence.
- *Setoff provisions.* Describes provisions for reducing the verdict amount to account for payments that the plaintiff has received from trusts, settling defendants, or parties that were not named in the case.

- *Indirect trust claims.* Reports the conditions that must be satisfied for a verdict defendant to bring a successful trust claim, according to the attorneys who practice in that state.

## California

### Liability Standard

Liability in California is joint and several for economic damages and several for noneconomic damages.[1] A defendant is liable if its products or practices were a substantial contributing factor to the injury.[2] There is no numerical definition (e.g., more than 1 percent of the exposure) of what it means to be a substantial contributing factor. The trier of fact will allocate a percentage of fault to each of the joint tortfeasors found liable and will establish the amount of recovery.[3]

### Assigning Fault to Trusts or Bankrupt Firms

Defendants can attempt to add potentially responsible parties (PRPs) to the verdict sheet. Bankrupt firms, parties that are shielded from liability (e.g., the Navy), and settling solvent parties can be included as PRPs.[4]

A plaintiffs' attorney who practices in California observed that defendants do put bankrupt firms on the verdict sheet when they have enough evidence and will also attempt to prove up a case against settling solvent parties. However, practices regarding PRPs appear to vary across defendants. One defense attorney reported that he seldom attempts to add a bankrupt firm to the verdict sheet because sufficient evidence is usually lacking. Defense attorneys also indicated that they typically do not attempt to add the nonsettling solvent parties to the verdict sheet. Some defendants are reluctant to add nonsettling solvent parties out of fear that these parties will turn around and name them in future cases.

### Timing of Trust Claims

There is no requirement regarding when a trust claim must be filed during the tort case. A prominent California plaintiffs' attorney said that he typically will delay filing until after trial.

---

[1] The Fair Responsibility Act of 1986, codified at California Civil Code §§ 1431–1431.2, established several liability for noneconomic damages.

[2] See, for example, *Rutherford*, 1997.

[3] California Code of Civil Procedure §§ 875–880. For rules about awards resulting from jury trials, see California Code of Civil Procedure §§ 624–630.

[4] See *DaFonte*, 1992 (holding that employers can be apportioned fault on a verdict sheet, even though they cannot be sued), and *Taylor*, 2003 (holding that the Navy can be assigned a share of the "fault" even though the Navy cannot be sued).

### Discoverability of Trust Claims

California judges have ruled that trust claim forms are discoverable.[5] Both plaintiff and defense attorneys agree that plaintiffs typically comply with defense requests to disclose claim forms, although the amount paid by the trust and any correspondence between the trust and the plaintiff regarding the settlement amount will not be disclosed. (The amount paid and correspondence regarding the settlement amount will likewise not be disclosed in settlements with solvent defendants.) Although plaintiffs do disclose claim forms that have been submitted, plaintiffs can avoid disclosing trust claims by waiting to file claims until after trial or until the case has settled.

Plaintiffs and defendants both indicated that there is seldom discovery related to settlements with solvent defendants. According to both plaintiffs and defendants, plaintiffs typically do not submit an affidavit of exposure in support of such settlements. Exposure affidavits would be the principal target of a discovery request.

### Admissibility of Trust Claims

Although trust claim forms are discoverable, admissibility is another matter.[6] According to a defense attorney, judges frequently deny admission. Even though a claim form can establish exposure to the product of a bankrupt firm, the claim form typically provides limited information on how much. Judges can then deny admission on the grounds that the claim form would be more prejudicial than probative.

### Setoff Provisions

Each verdict defendant is liable for its several share of the noneconomic damages and, thus, in most cases, is not entitled to a setoff credit for the portion of any settlement that is attributed to noneconomic damages.[7] It does not matter whether the payment is from a trust or a solvent party. For example, if a jury awards $3 million in noneconomic damages and assigns a particular defendant 5 percent of the fault, that defendant will owe $150,000 in noneconomic damages. The amount of previous settlements is immaterial. Plaintiffs bear the risk of entering a settlement that turns out to be less

---

[5] See *Volkswagen of America*, 2006. See also California Code of Civil Procedure § 2017.010 (on what matters are subject to discovery).

[6] See *Davies*, 1984, and *Glenfed Dev. Corp.*, 1997 (holding that the admissibility of evidence is not the test for the discoverability of information). See also California Evidence Code § 1152 ("Evidence that a person has, in compromise or from humanitarian motives, furnished or offered or promised to furnish money or any other thing, act, or service to another who has sustained or will sustain or claims that he or she has sustained or will sustain loss or damage, as well as any conduct or statements made in negotiation thereof, is inadmissible to prove his or her liability for the loss or damage or any part of it") and § 1154 ("Evidence that a person has accepted or offered or promised to accept a sum of money or any other thing, act, or service in satisfaction of a claim, as well as any conduct or statements made in negotiation thereof, is inadmissible to prove the invalidity of the claim or any part of it").

[7] See, e.g., *Garcia*, 2007.

than the liable party's proportionate share but reap the benefit of settlements that turn out to be greater than the proportionate share.

Setoffs are available for economic damages.[8] Between a week or so before trial and the time of the verdict, the judge will require the plaintiff to disclose the amount received in settlements from all sources. The bankruptcy status of the party making the payment is immaterial, and payments must be disclosed whether or not the settling party was named in the tort action. Payments made by bankruptcy trusts preverdict thus must be disclosed, as well as presuit settlements and settlements with solvent named defendants. The plaintiff reports the aggregate settlement amount to the judge—the names and amounts of the individual settlements are not detailed. The economic damages owed by the verdict defendants are reduced by the portion of the settlement attributed to economic damages, with the jury award used to determine the split between economic and noneconomic damages. Assume, for example, that the jury awarded $1 million in economic damages and $3 million in noneconomic damages and that settlements totaled $1 million. The verdict defendants would then receive a $250,000 setoff for economic damages and be liable for $750,000 in economic damages.

### Indirect Trust Claims

The California Code of Civil Procedure protects the right of joint tortfeasors to seek contribution when they pay a judgment in excess of their pro rata share.[9] Presumably, this would include the right of a verdict defendant to seek contribution for economic damages from a trust that has yet to pay the claimant. Plaintiff and defense attorneys differed over what they thought was required to bring a successful indirect trust claim once a verdict had been satisfied. A defense attorney argued that the jury would have to assign fault to the relevant bankrupt firm. A plaintiffs' lawyer argued instead that the defendant would have to supply only the same information that a direct claimant would have to supply if a direct claimant (plaintiff) were bringing the claim instead. Given that California is a single-satisfaction state, the same plaintiffs' attorney believed that full satisfaction of a verdict would enable a verdict defendant to bring an indirect claim for economic damages.

---

[8] California law allows for a reduction in any final judgment equal to the amount stipulated in a settlement, or in the amount of consideration paid for a settlement of liabilities, whichever is greater (California Code of Civil Procedure § 877).

[9] According to California Code of Civil Procedure § 875(c), "Such right of contribution may be enforced only after one tortfeasor has, by payment, discharged the joint judgment or has paid more than his pro rata share thereof. It shall be limited to the excess so paid over the pro rata share of the person so paying and in no event shall any tortfeasor be compelled to make contribution beyond his own pro rata share of the entire judgment." *Pro rata* means that if, for example, ten parties are assigned fault by the jury, each is held responsible for one-tenth of the economic damages regardless of the fault allocated to the individual parties.

A defense attorney observed that some trusts do not bar payment to the direct claimant when a verdict has been satisfied.[10] Indeed, a party very familiar with the operation of the Manville Trust indicated that a verdict does not extinguish a claimant's right to bring a claim against the Manville Trust.

Both plaintiff and defense attorneys were unaware of indirect contribution claims in California, reflecting in part the small number of verdicts.[11] Indirect contribution claims have not been filed, according to defense attorneys, because the amount available for recovery is not large enough to be worth pursuing.

## Illinois

### Liability Standard

Liability is joint and several for both economic and noneconomic damages in Illinois.[12] An asbestos defendant is jointly and severally liable if the plaintiff can show that the defendant was responsible for at least 1 percent of the plaintiff's asbestos exposure. Punitive damages are available but, according to attorneys with whom we spoke, have not been imposed for many years. The jury will assign a percentage of fault to the defendants at trial and will also assign a percentage of fault to the plaintiff if the plaintiff contributed to the harm (percentages sum to 100 percent). If the plaintiff is found to be more than 50 percent at fault, the case against the defendants is dismissed.[13] If the plaintiff is found to be between 0 and 50 percent at fault, the award is reduced by the percentage of fault assigned to the plaintiff.

### Assigning Fault to Trusts or Bankrupt Firms

Only the parties at trial can be put on the verdict sheet. Neither settling solvent parties nor any entity not named in the lawsuit can be apportioned a share of liability on an Illinois verdict sheet. Both plaintiff and defense attorneys who practice in Illinois indicated that neither bankrupt firms nor trusts can be named in the case or appear on the verdict sheet.[14] Even though a liability share cannot be allocated to a bankrupt firm, a

---

[10] However, a plaintiffs' attorney cautioned that the verdict would have to address all potential causes of action—including personal injury, wrongful death, and loss of consortium.

[11] Indirect contribution claims should be distinguished from indirect indemnity claims. Contribution applies when one party has paid part of the liability of another party. Indemnity applies in this context when a contractual arrangement between two parties indemnifies one party from liability (for example, when the manufacturer of asbestos-containing products indemnifies a distributor from liability).

[12] 735 ILCS 5/2-1118.

[13] 735 ILCS 5/2-1116(c).

[14] See *Ready*, 2008 (in which the Supreme Court of Illinois held that settling parties should not be listed on Illinois verdict forms).

defendant has the right to use information on exposure to a bankrupt firm's products to show that it was not a significant contributing factor to the injury.[15]

### Timing of Trust Claims

Under Illinois law, there is no requirement regarding when a plaintiff must file a trust claim. There were differing perceptions as to when plaintiffs file trust claims in Illinois. Defense lawyers claimed that plaintiffs typically do not file trust claims until the case has been closed. Plaintiffs' attorneys, on the other hand, reported that they usually bring claims early on in a case.

### Discoverability of Trust Claims

The attorneys interviewed indicated that disclosure of trust claim forms is not part of standard master discovery orders.[16] However, plaintiffs' attorneys reported that judges will usually grant requests for disclosure of trust claims. Defense attorneys complain that plaintiffs often refuse to disclose trust claim forms even when they have been ordered to do so. Defendants must then petition the court to enforce the order. Thus, from the defendants' point of view, trust claim forms are in theory obtainable but are very difficult to obtain in Illinois.

### Admissibility of Trust Claims

Trust claims are not automatically admissible into evidence.[17] It is up to the judge to determine whether a claim form can be admitted. As with any other piece of proposed evidence, the judge must determine that the information contained in the trust claim forms is relevant to the case. Plaintiffs' attorneys pointed out that a claim form does not necessarily provide evidence that a plaintiff was exposed to the debtor's product.

### Setoff Provisions

Verdict defendants receive pro tanto setoffs for all settlements and other payments related to the injury.[18] The verdict is reduced dollar for dollar by the amount of payments, and verdict defendants are jointly and severally liable for the remainder.[19] The

[15] *Nolan*, 2009.

[16] See Illinois Supreme Court Rules, Rule 201. The standard asbestos interrogatory for Madison County that was issued in January 2011 by Judge Barbara Crowder directs plaintiffs to "state the name and address of the person, entity and/or trust, the date the claim or suit was filed, the nature of the injury, whether the claim or suit is presently pending, the amount of money you received, if any, and/or the amount of money that has been pledged." However, it does not direct plaintiffs to disclose the trust claim forms ("Standard Asbestos Interrogatories Directed to Plaintiffs," *In re all asbestos litigation filed in Madison County*, 2011).

[17] See Illinois Rules of Evidence, Article IV (on relevancy of evidence and limits thereon).

[18] Illinois Joint Tortfeasor Contribution Act, 740 ILCS 100/2(c).

[19] If a trust has settled a claim but has not made payment before the setoff is calculated, the payment is assigned to the verdict defendants.

bankruptcy status of the party making the payment is immaterial, and payments must be disclosed regardless of whether the settling party was named in the tort action. Plaintiffs are not formally required to disclose the amount received until after a verdict has been reached. The plaintiff will disclose the aggregate amount received, not itemize the individual settlements.

In order to encourage settlements, an experienced plaintiffs' attorney reported that judges frequently ask the plaintiff to disclose the amount received prior to trial. Although this plaintiffs' attorney did not believe that such a request would be legally enforceable, he complies with such a request in order to remain in the good graces of the judge.

#### Indirect Trust Claims

Any verdict defendant that pays a joint tortfeasor's share of tort liability receives a right to contribution.[20] Both plaintiff and defense attorneys agreed that, once a verdict has been paid, the defendant can stand in the shoes of the plaintiff and bring claims against the trusts. According to the plaintiff side, there is no need for the plaintiff to assign trust recovery rights to the defendant, and there is no need for the trust or bankrupt firm to be found liable (bankrupt firms cannot be found liable in any case). Plaintiffs are not required to cooperate with or assist defendants in filing claims with the trusts post-verdict as they are in West Virginia.

### New York

#### Liability Standard

Liability in New York is joint and several for economic damages. If a defendant is found to be 50 percent or less at fault, liability for that defendant is several for non-economic damages.[21] Nevertheless, a defendant will be jointly and severally liable for noneconomic damages if that defendant is found to have acted recklessly or to have acted in concert with other parties to conceal the dangers of asbestos.[22] According to a plaintiffs' attorney who practices in New York, his firm is typically successful in establishing recklessness. The jury will allocate fault to the parties at trial and to the so-called nonparties potentially liable.

A defense attorney observed that punitive damages are not allowed in New York City but are available in other parts of New York state.

---

[20] 740 ILCS 100/2(f).

[21] New York Civil Practice Law and Rules, Article 16 § 1601. According to plaintiffs' attorneys who practice in New York, it is very rare for a single defendant to be found more than 50 percent at fault.

[22] New York Civil Practice Law and Rules, Article 16 §§ 1601(7) and (11).

Plaintiffs' attorneys indicated that they often decline to seek economic damages in New York City asbestos cases. Plaintiffs are concerned that the jury will tie the non-economic award to the economic award and believe that the resulting decrease in non-economic damages will more than offset any economic damages awarded. A defense attorney estimated that plaintiffs seek economic damages in less than 10 percent of cases.

### Assigning Fault to Trusts or Bankrupt Firms

Defendants can add bankrupt firms, solvent parties that have settled out of the case, and any other party not named in the case to the verdict sheet.[23] In order to do so, however, defendants must prove up a case against these potentially liable nonparties. Defendants must make a prima facie case that a nonparty contributed to the plaintiff's asbestos exposure, the exposure contributed to the plaintiff's injury, and the party failed to warn or was negligent in some way.

According to one plaintiffs' attorney, defendants are often successful in adding bankrupt firms to the verdict sheet. Defendants, however, emphasize how difficult it is to prove up a case against bankrupt firms. In their experience, trust claims, even if available to the defendant, are usually not enough: The claim form might be sufficient to establish that the plaintiff's injury was caused by asbestos and, in some cases, might be sufficient to establish exposure to the bankrupt firm's asbestos-containing products. However, it will not show that the bankrupt firm failed to warn or knew or should have known about the dangers of asbestos. In addition, defendants complain that plaintiffs' attorneys coach their clients not to recall exposure to the products of bankrupt firms during deposition. Defendants maintain that it is difficult for them to identify co-workers who could testify about exposure to insolvents' products. Plaintiffs' attorneys respond that they do not just simply rely on their clients' memories but spend considerable effort to assemble invoices, shipping orders, and other documents that can prove liability. They see no reason why defense attorneys cannot do the same. Plaintiffs' attorneys also strongly object to the implication that their clients hide the truth.

### Timing of Trust Claims

A case management order that applies to asbestos cases filed in New York City requires plaintiffs to file all trust claims 90 days before trial in in extremis cases for living plaintiffs with very severe asbestos diseases, and no later than ten days after a case is assigned to a first-in, first-out (FIFO) trial cluster for cases on the FIFO (or "active") docket.[24]

---

23 See *N.Y. City Asbestos Litig.*, 2004. But also see Shelley, Cohn, and Arnold, 2008, p. 269: "[W]hile Rule 1601 permits asbestos-supplying tortfeasors to be included on the verdict sheet for purposes of allocating shares of responsibility, if a bankrupt entity were considered to be a culpable party over which the plaintiff could not obtain jurisdiction, solvent defendants might not be permitted to factor in the shares of the bankrupt entities' responsibility and might be forced to effectively reallocate those shares among themselves."

24 *N.Y. City Asbestos Litigation*, Amended Case Management Order, Index 40000/88, as of February 19, 2003.

One plaintiffs' attorney, however, did not believe that New York courts could legally enforce this requirement, and defense attorneys indicated that it was not routinely complied with.[25] Defense attorneys observed that plaintiffs typically wait to file trust claims until after depositions are complete or until after the case has been resolved. The New York plaintiffs' attorneys with whom we spoke, on the other hand, believed that the benefit of distributing money to their clients outweighs any potential strategic advantage to delaying trust filings. Their declared practice is thus to file trust claims as soon as the information needed to complete the claim form becomes available.

### Discoverability of Trust Claims

The asbestos case management order for New York City was amended in 2005 to require disclosure of trust claim forms.[26] Plaintiffs' attorneys indicated that they routinely turn over trust claim forms to defendants. Some defense attorneys believe that plaintiffs' attorneys fail to or only partially comply with the disclosure requirement. They point to examples in which a plaintiffs' firm denied that trust claims had been filed but in which it was later discovered that claims had been filed prior to the denial.[27]

### Admissibility of Trust Claims

Defense attorneys indicated that they have been able to introduce claim forms into evidence in some cases. Defense attorneys find that the trust claim forms are often sufficient to prove exposure to the insolvent's products but not to establish fault. Defense attorneys noted that the information required by some trusts is not even enough to establish exposure to the bankrupt firm's products or practices. Plaintiffs' attorneys observed that claim forms might not be admissible.

### Setoff Provisions

Because plaintiffs in New York reportedly seek economic damages in a small percentage of cases, we focus our attention on setoffs for noneconomic damages. Prior to the trial, the plaintiff is required to disclose all payments pertaining to the injury recovered from or promised or pledged by any person or entity.[28] The verdict defendants receive a setoff that is the greater of the aggregate amount received and the aggregate share

[25] In *Canella* (2008), the judge directed the plaintiff to file trust claims if he planned to file any and said that she would vacate a defense verdict if trust claims were filed post-verdict. Plaintiffs' attorneys complained that the judge was "ordering us to file something [trust claims] which we don't know if we are going to file or not."

[26] See New York City Asbestos Litigation Defendants' Standard Article 16 Interrogatories and Request for Production of Documents (*In re New York City Asbestos Litigation*, 2003).

[27] Failure to disclose trust claims is not necessarily intentional. In some cases, trust claims are filed by a referring (or intake) law firm but the discovery responses coordinated by the litigating firm. The litigating firm might be unaware of whether the referring firm has filed claims; however, one might argue that it is the litigating firm's duty to keep up with trust claim filings made by the referring firm.

[28] New York General Obligations Law § 15-108(a).

of fault assigned to the settling parties. If the plaintiff receives payment from a party but the jury does not find the party at fault, the payment is included in the aggregate amount received, but the aggregate share of fault does not increase because the share of fault of this party is effectively zero.

Consider the following example:

- The jury awards $1 million in noneconomic damages.
- Defendant 1 has not settled and is found 40 percent at fault.
- Defendant 2 settles pretrial for $150,000 and is found 30 percent at fault.
- Defendant 3 has not settled and is found 30 percent at fault.
- Party 4 has paid $500,000 to the plaintiff but was not assigned liability by the jury.

Liability is several for the noneconomic damages because no defendant is more than 50 percent at fault and none has been found reckless. The aggregate amount received in settlements is $650,000, which is greater than the amount corresponding to aggregate fault of the settling parties ($300,000 or 30 percent of $1 million). The plaintiff is thus allowed to recover only $350,000 of the verdict. Several liability limits the potential payments by defendants 1 and 3 to $400,000 and $300,000, respectively. The plaintiff could recover the entire $350,000 from defendant 1, $300,000 from defendant 3, and the remaining $50,000 from defendant 1, or fashion some other combination of recoveries that satisfies the constraints on recoveries from defendants 1 and 3. If the jury had found defendant 3 reckless, the plaintiff could recover the entire $350,000 from defendant 3 because defendant 3 is now jointly and severally liable. Defendant 3 could then recover $50,000 from defendant 1, the excess of defendant 3's payment over its assigned share of the fault.

### Indirect Trust Claims

New York law entitles verdict defendants to seek contribution from joint tortfeasors.[29] One defense attorney believed that certain conditions would need to be satisfied in order to successfully bring an indirect trust claim seeking contribution for a verdict paid by a solvent defendant. First, the defendant would need to be found jointly and severally liable. If a defendant were only severally liable, then it would have no right to contribution because it would not be required to pay more than its share of the judgment. Second, the jury would have to assign fault to the relevant bankrupt firm for an indirect claim to be successful. It is only when fault is assigned to the bankrupt firm that the defendant can show that it paid the bankrupt firm's share. Third, the defendant would have to pay the bankrupt firm's share of the award.

---

[29] New York General Obligations Law § 14-1401-2.

What happens in cases in which a defendant has been found jointly and severally liable and the bankrupt firm has not been assigned fault? The New York plaintiffs' attorneys with whom we spoke argued that, if the verdict had been paid in full, they would not attempt to recover from asbestos trusts. They believed that because New York is a single-satisfaction state, it would not be appropriate to seek trust recovery. Even if TDPs are unclear about whether recovery is permitted under such circumstances, the plaintiffs' attorneys argued that recovery would be unethical and attempts at trust recovery would damage the firm's reputation. Thus, the plaintiffs' attorneys indicated that they would not attempt to recover when a verdict has been paid in full and the insolvent party has not been named. As reported in the previous paragraph, New York defense attorneys believed that the defendants that paid the verdict would not be able to recover from the trust in such a situation either.

The defense attorneys interviewed who practiced in New York indicated that they were not aware of any indirect trust claims resulting from New York tort cases.

## Pennsylvania

### Liability Standard

Until recently, liability has been joint and several for both economic and noneconomic damages in Pennsylvania.[30] Under a law enacted on June 28, 2011, liability for asbestos injuries is now several, with some exceptions.[31] Cases in which the plaintiff knew or should have known prior to June 28, 2011, that he or she was injured remain subject to joint-and-several liability. Our analysis applies to cases that are subject to this *prior* liability regime.

In cases subject to joint-and-several liability, plaintiffs typically seek to establish strict liability in asbestos cases.[32] When liability is strict, the jury does not allocate a percentage of fault to each of the liable defendants. Rather, each party is held liable for an equal share of the verdict (a pro rata share). In negligence suits, alternatively, each defendant is held liable for that proportion of the total dollar amount awarded as damages "in the ratio of the amount of [its] causal negligence to the amount of causal negligence attributed to all defendants against [which] recovery is allowed."[33]

---

30 See, e.g., *Crowell*, 1992. See also 42 Pa. Con. Stat. §7102(b).

31 Levy, 2011.

32 Plaintiffs will often begin a case by asserting both strict liability and negligence. They may keep both causes of action alive until trial and then jettison the negligence case.

33 Pennsylvania Comparative Negligence Act, 42 Pa. Con. Stat. § 7102(b).

### Assigning Fault to Trusts or Bankrupt Firms

In Pennsylvania, bankrupt firms cannot be included on the verdict sheet and thus cannot be found liable by the jury.[34] A trust can be listed on the verdict sheet if permitted by the trust documents. The Manville Trust is one such trust. The relevant part of Manville's TDPs reads as follows:

> Third-party claims may be asserted against the Trust for the sole purpose of listing the Trust on a verdict form or otherwise as necessary to ensure that any verdict reduction in respect of the Manville (or Trust) liability share is made pursuant to applicable law. No objection shall be made by the Trust or the claimant to the filing by a Co-Defendant of a third-party complaint or to the joinder of the Trust for this limited purpose only. (Manville Personal Injury Settlement Trust, 2010, Section I[1][c])

The Manville Trust has been named in Pennsylvania cases (see, for example, *Baker*, 2000). We have not been able to search the documents of other trusts for similar language, but, according to attorneys who practice in Pennsylvania, only one or two other older trusts contain similar language. Thus, the vast majority of trusts cannot be named in a case or included on the verdict sheet.[35]

Even if defendants are able to name a trust, both plaintiffs' attorneys and defense attorneys reported that they do not. As is discussed later in this appendix, setoffs for trust payments are pro tanto, and these pro tanto setoffs create disincentives for defendants to include trusts on the verdict sheet. For example, consider a situation in which four parties have been found liable for a $1 million verdict and that three of the parties have settled pre-verdict. The settling parties will typically require a pro rata release to protect them from future contribution claims from nonsettling defendants. Pro rata releases in this example meant that the remaining defendant will be liable for $250,000 (regardless of what the three settling defendants actually paid). Now add the Manville Trust to the verdict sheet and assume that Manville pays $50,000 to the plaintiff. The pro rata share for each of the five parties is $200,000. The setoff for the Manville payments is $50,000, so the nonsettling defendant now pays $200,000 + $200,000 – $50,000, or $350,000. The nonsettling defendant is worse off when Manville is assigned fault than when it is not.

Settled parties can be included on the verdict sheet in Pennsylvania. If the plaintiff does not concede the liability of the settling party, defendants that remain solvent

---

[34] *Ottavio*, 1992; *Sealover*, 1993 ("*Ottavio* stands for the complementary propositions that juries should apportion liability only among solvent defendants while bankrupt defendants should not appear on verdict sheets"). The recent changes in Pennsylvania liability law contain provisions that might allow trusts to be assigned fault under some conditions.

[35] See also *Ottavio*, 1992, p. 293 (favorably citing 2d Cir. precedent barring the Manville Trust from being listed as a potential tortfeasor on a verdict form).

must prove up a case against the settling party in order to have it listed on the verdict sheet. According to one defense attorney, plaintiffs often concede liability in order to avoid any focus at trial on asbestos exposures other than those caused by the trial defendants.

### Timing of Trust Claims

With the exception of Montgomery County, there is no requirement in Pennsylvania regarding when a plaintiff must file a trust claim. In Montgomery County, plaintiffs must file "any and all Asbestos Bankruptcy Trust claims available to him or her" 120 days prior to trial.[36] The requirement applies to all cases pending as of February 22, 2010, as well as cases subsequently filed. It is too soon to assess the impact of this new case management order.

According to defense attorneys who practice in Philadelphia, plaintiffs typically wait to submit trust claims until after the case has settled or a verdict has been entered. Defense attorneys also find that the trust claims that are submitted prior to trial are often filed only to comply with a trust's statute of limitations and are frequently incomplete.

### Discoverability of Trust Claims

According to one defense attorney who practices in Philadelphia, Judge Sandra Moss (the asbestos judge in Philadelphia) requires plaintiffs to disclose trust filings as part of the standard discovery process. Plaintiffs are required to disclose claim forms and any additional exposure information that the plaintiff has filed with the trust. Disclosure is due 120 days before trial, and plaintiffs are required to update the information prior to trial.[37] Any payment received from the trusts is not required to be disclosed until a verdict has been reached.[38] According to a plaintiffs' attorney who practices primarily in western Pennsylvania, plaintiffs provide trust claims to defendants when requested. When the claims are disclosed varies by jurisdiction, but, much of the time, it is done following deposition of the plaintiff by the defense.

### Admissibility of Trust Claims

In Pennsylvania, whether a claim form can be admitted into evidence depends on the facts of the case. The attorneys we interviewed were aware of multiple cases in which the trial judge allowed claim forms to be admitted. These claim forms were typically

---

36 *Thibeault*, 2010, p. 3. Montgomery County covers parts of suburban Philadelphia.

37 Judge Moss signed an amendment to *In re Asbestos Litigation* on April 5, 2010, that required plaintiffs to respond to defense interrogatories on bankruptcy trusts (which includes disclosure of trust claim forms and exposure evidence) within 30 days of the defense request (*In re Asbestos Litigation*, 2010).

38 According to several defense attorneys, defendants did not start requesting trust claim forms in Pennsylvania until 2007 or 2008. Prior to that time, there were not enough trusts to warrant the effort.

not used to put a trust on the verdict sheet. Rather, they were used, for example, to show that the plaintiff was exposed to amphibole asbestos rather than the chrysotile asbestos in a particular defendant's product. In other cases, judges have ruled that a claim form is not detailed enough to be admitted into evidence. A judge might determine, for example, that, even though a claim form shows that a plaintiff was at a particular worksite, it might not provide sufficient information to conclude that the plaintiff was exposed to a bankrupt firm's product.

### Setoff Provisions

Pennsylvania provides setoffs for payments made by parties deemed to be joint tortfeasors.[39] Thus, payments by trusts that are not found liable do not enter the setoff calculation. Because, with few exceptions, trusts cannot be named in a case or appear on the verdict sheet, defendants will not receive setoffs for prejudgment trust payments in most cases. There is also no provision under Pennsylvania law or court procedure to reduce judgments for trust payments made after a judgment has been entered.

A recent lower court opinion in Philadelphia County suggests that setoff practices for trust payments may be in a state of flux. In *Reed* (2010), the court reduced the verdict to reflect payments by several trusts that were not found to be joint tortfeasors. Whether this decision will be followed by other judges or confirmed on appeal remains to be seen.

The type of setoff depends on the language of the release.[40] If the settlement is silent, the setoff defaults to pro tanto.[41] Settling solvent defendants typically insist on a pro rata release because that is the only way they will be protected from contribution claims by verdict defendants. When the setoff is pro rata, a plaintiff's ultimate recovery against the verdict defendants is reduced by pro rata shares of the settling solvent defendants who are assigned liability. Consider, for example, a $1 million verdict with four liable parties. Further assume that three of the defendants are solvent and settled prior to trial. The remaining verdict defendant will receive a $250,000 setoff for each of the solvent settling defendants, regardless of how much they settled for. The amount

---

39 Pennsylvania Uniform Contribution Among Tortfeasors Act, 42 Pa. Con. Stat. § 8322. See also *Baker*, 2000 ("a non-settling defendant is not entitled to a set-off in light of the settling defendant's release unless the settling and non-settling defendants are both deemed to be joint tortfeasors"). In addition, in at least one case, Pennsylvania courts have allowed setoffs for money due to plaintiffs but yet to be paid by a bankruptcy trust. See *Andaloro*, 2002.

40 See 42 Pa. Con. Stat. § 8325 ("A release by the injured person of one joint tort-feasor, whether before or after judgment, does not discharge the other tort-feasors unless the release so provides, but reduces the claim against the other tort-feasors in the amount of the consideration paid for the release or in any amount or proportion by which the release provides that the total claim shall be reduced if greater than the consideration paid").

41 "[I]f the settlement agreement is silent, the set off mechanism defaults to a pro tanto set off and the nonsettling defendant is entitled to have the verdict reduced by the amount of consideration paid by the settling tortfeasor" (*Baker*, 2000, p. 667).

paid by the settling solvent defendants is therefore not relevant and need not be disclosed by the plaintiff.

The Manville Trust documents specify that the setoff amount should be either the liquidated trust payment or the trust's pro rata share of the judgment as provided by state law.[42] In the 2000 *Baker* case, the Pennsylvania Supreme Court determined that setoff for payments by the Manville Trust should equal the amount paid (pro tanto setoff), not the pro rata share of the trust. There is some uncertainty whether the *Baker* case applies to other trusts; however, the *Baker* court concluded that, if a settlement agreement is silent on whether the setoff is pro tanto or pro rata, the nonsettling party is entitled to only a pro tanto setoff.

#### Indirect Trust Claims

Claims for contribution are allowed in Pennsylvania for joint tortfeasors that have paid more than their pro rata share.[43] There was a difference of opinion between plaintiff and defense lawyers over what is required for an indirect trust claim to be successful. Several defense lawyers with whom we spoke believed that the trust would have to have been found liable. Another defense lawyer thought that a verdict defendant might be able to recover from a trust if the plaintiff identified the bankrupt firm in the deposition. In contrast, a Pennsylvania plaintiffs' attorney believed that, when a verdict was satisfied, the bankrupt firm or trust would not need to be found liable for an indirect claim to succeed, but would need to satisfy only the claim-approval criteria established for direct claimants. The plaintiffs' attorney also believed that the plaintiff would not be able to bring a trust claim at some trusts once a judgment had been fully satisfied.

### Texas

#### Liability Standard

Liability for toxic-tort cases in Texas is several when the defendant is 50 percent or less responsible for the injury. A defendant is jointly and severally liable if he or she is more than 50 percent at fault.[44] According to one plaintiffs' attorney who tries asbestos cases in Texas, it is very rare for a defendant to be found more than 50 percent at fault. He was aware of no such cases since the Borg-Warner decision was issued in June 2007. For all practical purposes, liability for both economic and noneconomic damages is thus several in Texas asbestos cases.

---

[42] Manville Personal Injury Settlement Trust, 2010, I(3)(c)(i).

[43] 42 Pa. Con. Stat. § 8324.

[44] Texas Civ. Prac. & Rem. Code Ann., Title 2, Ch. 33, §33.013(b) (2009). The cutoff for several liability was 10 percent prior to 1997 and 15 percent between 1997 and 2003 (per Former Tex. Civ. Prac. & Rem. Code §33.013[c][2]).

### Assigning Fault to Trusts or Bankrupt Firms

Section 33.003 of the Texas Civil Practice and Remedies Code requires the trier of fact to allocate a percentage of responsibility to each claimant, each defendant, each settling person, and each RTP. Defendants can designate RTPs in a case and attempt to add them to the verdict sheet. RTPs can include bankrupt firms and parties otherwise exempt from liability.[45] A plaintiff can make a no-evidence summary-judgment motion to prevent a bankrupt firm from being included on the verdict sheet as an RTP. To defeat the summary-judgment motion, defendants must meet the *Borg-Warner* evidentiary standards as interpreted by Judge Mark Davidson (the multidistrict litigation asbestos judge in Texas). Judge Davidson requires defendants to quantify exposure in some way—for example, by establishing the frequency and duration of exposure.[46]

Both plaintiffs and defendants indicated that it is very difficult to meet the *Borg-Warner* standards. Trust claims alone do not provide enough information to satisfy *Borg-Warner.* Trust claims might show that the plaintiff was at a site but will typically not provide the information necessary to establish the frequency and duration of exposure or quantify the dose. Prominent Texas plaintiffs' attorney Steve Baron commented on the nature of exposure information in trust claims during a hearing on RTPs before Judge Davidson on October 16, 2008. Baron explains,

> Interestingly, the [trust] claim form and what you must prove, you don't even have to prove exposure. . . . The trusts readily acknowledge [that their] products were at many, many job sites and they give you the list. . . . If you worked at one, all you have to say is, I worked there. That is all. End of inquiry. No more statements. No more allegations.[47]

Baron continues,

> Now in order to get paid [from a trust], I had to submit statements, whatever it is, proof, you bet they [the defendants in a tort case] can use that against me. Of course, they can. But it doesn't in and of itself—a box that I checked that said I

---

[45] Per the 1995 amendments to the Texas Code, RTPs expressly did not include "a person or entity that is a debtor in bankruptcy proceedings or a person or entity against whom this claimant's claim has been discharged in bankruptcy, except to the extent that liability insurance or other source of third party funding may be available to pay claims asserted against the debtor" (former Tex. Civ. Prac. & Rem. Code §33.011[6][B][ii]). We have not investigated whether the exception in this definition would apply to companies that are reorganized under Section 524(g) of the bankruptcy code. However, amendments to the code in 2003 removed this restrictive definition of RTPs.

[46] Davidson, 2009. The 2007 *Borg-Warner* decision is directed at a plaintiff trying to prove up a case against a defendant. Judge Davidson has applied the decision to defendants seeking to include RTPs in asbestos cases. One plaintiffs' attorney commented that the evidence that *Borg-Warner* requires is not available anywhere—for either plaintiffs or defendants. He believed that the *Borg-Warner* decision was an important reason for the decline in asbestos litigation in Texas over the past several years.

[47] Baron, 2008, pp. 158–159.

> worked at Exxon and here is my pathology report, certainly doesn't stop me from denying that they have the level of proof required in Texas to hold that trust on as a responsible third party.[48]

As a result of the stringent evidentiary standards, defense attorneys reported that they do not attempt to list all bankrupt firms as RTPs but rather focus on the ones that appear to be responsible for the largest exposures. Plaintiffs' attorneys indicated that it is common for bankrupt firms to be listed on the verdict sheet, but, since Judge Davidson's interpretation of the *Borg-Warner* decision, fewer and fewer have been listed.

Defendants can also designate settling solvent defendants as RTPs. In principle, a plaintiff could also file a no-evidence summary judgment that would force the remaining defendants to meet the *Borg-Warner* standard for these parties. According to defense attorneys who practice in Texas, however, plaintiffs do not challenge the RTP designation of settled solvent defendants. One defense attorney speculated that plaintiffs do not make such challenges because doing so would, in effect, require them to maintain that there was sufficient proof against the settling solvent defendant to ward off a no-evidence summary-judgment motion prior to the settlement and then take the position that there was no *Borg-Warner* evidence once the settlement was concluded. The result is that settled solvent defendants in Texas typically end up on the verdict sheet but trusts that have made pre-verdict payments do not.

#### Timing of Trust Claims

There is no requirement in Texas for when trust claims must be filed. Plaintiffs' attorneys with whom we spoke reported that the decision on when to file a trust claim is based in part on the financial condition of their client. It is also based on an assessment of how claim filing might affect the tort case. Plaintiffs' attorneys indicated that they would delay filing if they believed that the information would assist the defendants in assigning liability to RTPs. Plaintiffs' attorneys are worried that defense attorneys will misconstrue the information in a trust claim filing in order to inappropriately increase the share of fault assigned to bankrupt firms.

Defense attorneys indicated that they rarely receive trust claim forms because plaintiffs delay filing until the case has been resolved.

#### Discoverability of Trust Claims

The master discovery rule for asbestos cases requires plaintiffs to disclose claim forms. Judge Davidson requires trust claim forms to be disclosed 60 days before trial. Plaintiffs are required to disclose all information in the trust submissions related to exposure but not materials related to the settlement amount. The master discovery rule also requires plaintiffs to identify the trusts from which they plan to seek recovery.

---

[48] Baron, 2008, pp. 161–162.

Defendants note, however, that this part of the rule is of little value because plaintiffs' attorneys typically respond that they will evaluate potential trust claims once the tort case has been resolved.

### Admissibility of Trust Claims

Admissibility of trust claims is up to the judge. The attorneys interviewed were not aware of any Texas law or controlling authority that addressed the admission of claim forms.

### Setoff Provisions

Plaintiffs are required to disclose all settlements paid in consideration of the injury at issue, typically 60 days before trial. Payments must be disclosed regardless of whether the settling party has been found liable and regardless of whether the party has been named in the case or alleged to be an RTP. In most cases, the plaintiff is required to disclose the names of the parties providing payment and the aggregate amount paid. Plaintiffs are not required to estimate potential future recoveries from trusts.

When liability is several, the parties are liable only for their allocated share of fault, subject to the proviso that the total recovery is not greater than the verdict.[49] Consider, for example, a $1 million verdict with five parties that are each found 20 percent responsible. Also assume that four of the parties settled prior to trial for a total of $500,000. The remaining defendant will be required to pay $200,000, and the plaintiff will consequently recover $700,000. The plaintiff bears the risk of settlements that are less than the share of fault assigned to the settling parties. Now assume that the four parties settled for $900,000. The remaining defendant will then be required to pay only $100,000 because a payment in excess of $100,000 would cause the total amount recovered to exceed the verdict amount.

### Indirect Trust Claims

Contribution claims for joint liability are governed by Chapter 32 of the Texas Code. When liability is several, the verdict defendant has no basis for an indirect claim against a trust. The verdict defendant pays only its share of the award and cannot recover from a trust because it has not satisfied any obligation that a trust might have to the plaintiff.

Plaintiffs' attorneys believe that plaintiffs would likely be able to recover from some trusts even if the verdict was paid in full.[50] The plaintiff would retain the right to file a trust claim because no defendant had satisfied any obligation the trust might have to the plaintiff. Even if the defendant had not been successful in assigning fault to

---

49 Texas Civ. Prac. & Rem. Code Ann., Title 2, Ch. 33, §33.012. Because the 50-percent fault threshold makes it very difficult to hold a party jointly and severally liable, we restrict our attention to situations in which liability is several.

50 Some trusts will not pay a claim if a judgment has been paid in full (see Chapter Two).

the bankrupt firm, the plaintiff might still succeed in recovering from the trust because the standards for recovery from the trust differ from those needed to prove up a case against an RTP.

## West Virginia

### Liability Standard

Prior to July 2005, liability in asbestos personal injury cases was joint and several in West Virginia. In July 2005, a new statute took effect that restricts joint-and-several liability to defendants that are more than 30 percent at fault. However, some exceptions to this restriction are provided. In particular, joint-and-several liability applies to "[a]ny party strictly liable for the manufacture and sale of a defective product."[51] Both defense and plaintiff attorneys with whom we spoke believed that asbestos falls under this exception and that liability remains joint and several regardless of the percentage of fault assigned to a defendant.[52] The attorneys, however, were unaware of any asbestos cases that had reached verdict since the statute went into effect, so the statute's provisions remain untested for asbestos cases.

### Assigning Fault to Trusts or Bankrupt Firms

Section 55-7-24 of the West Virginia Code directs the trial court to instruct the jury to determine the "proportionate fault of each party in the litigation at the time the verdict was rendered." An earlier decision by the West Virginia Supreme Court addressed the allocation of liability among joint tortfeasors. In the 1982 *Sitzes* opinion, the court wrote

> Because the right of comparative contribution is designed for the benefit of defendant joint tortfeasors, it can only be invoked by one of the joint tortfeasors in the litigation. The method for invoking the right on comparative contribution is by requesting that special interrogatories pursuant to Rule 49(b) of the West Virginia Rules of Civil Procedure be given to the jury requiring it to allocate the various joint tortfeasors' degree of primary fault. . . . In the absence of such request, all joint tortfeasors, who are parties to the action are found to be liable to the plaintiff, [and] will then share in the total judgment on a pro rata basis according to the number found liable.[53]

---

[51] West Virginia Code § 55-7-24.

[52] The *Morningstar* (1979) decision establishes strict liability for product-liability cases in West Virginia.

[53] *Sitzes*, 1982, p. 688.

Thus, defendants in asbestos personal injury cases can request an allocation of fault among the joint tortfeasors. The issue is whether bankrupt firms or trusts can be considered joint tortfeasors.

West Virginia rules are not clear regarding whether bankrupt firms or the trusts can be on the verdict sheet. Case law has allowed apportionment of fault and setoffs to solvent parties that are not named in the lawsuit; however, whether trusts or bankrupt firms can be entered on verdict forms has not yet been fully addressed by West Virginia courts.[54] A defense attorney with whom we spoke gave an example of a judge who allowed the jury to allocate fault to an "other" category. The jury could, in principle, assign fault for the bankrupt firms to this category. In his view, however, whether bankrupt firms or trusts can be on the verdict sheet remains an open question. Plaintiffs' attorneys who practice argue that the channeling injunction prevents bankrupt firms from being named in the suit and thus that bankrupt firms are not parties to the litigation. There are no provisions for allocating liability in West Virginia to what are sometimes referred to as RTPs in other states. Plaintiffs thus argue that fault cannot be assigned to bankrupt firms or trusts in West Virginia. Again, there have been no asbestos verdicts since July 2005 to test these theories.

Settling solvent parties are not included on the verdict sheet. There is no need to do so because setoffs are provided for all settlements paid in consideration of the injury at issue. There would analogously be no need to include bankrupt firms of trusts that have made payments to the plaintiff.

### Timing of Trust Claims

There are no requirements for when a trust claim must be filed in West Virginia. A plaintiffs' attorney who practices in West Virginia stated that his firm files trust claims as soon as the required information becomes available and the trust is open. One defense attorney reported that, by the time a case reaches trial, plaintiffs' attorneys will typically have filed claims with some trusts for which their client is eligible but not with others.

### Discoverability of Trust Claims

A March 2010 case management order for West Virginia asbestos claims requires that, no later than 120 days before trial, asbestos personal injury plaintiffs provide

> all parties a statement of any and all existing claims that may exist against asbestos trusts. In addition, the statement shall also disclose when a claim was or will be made, and whether there has been any request for deferral, delay, suspension or tolling of the asbestos trust claim process. The statement must contain an Affidavit

---

[54] See *Louk*, 1996, p. 927 n. 14. Also see Shelley, Cohn, and Arnold, 2008, p. 268.

of the Plaintiff or Plaintiff's counsel that the statement is based upon a good faith investigation of *all potential claims* against asbestos trusts.[55]

What it means to do "a good faith investigation of all potential claims" is open to interpretation, but one could argue that it does not require all trust claims to be filed 120 days before trial—rather, only that the potential for such claims has been investigated. With regard to claims that have already been filed, the plaintiff must disclose the claim forms, as well as "any supporting materials used to support" the claim. Subsequent to the 120-day cutoff, plaintiffs must disclose any additional information that supports filing of additional trust claims within 30 days of the receipt of the information but, in no event, later than the commencement of the trial.[56] A defense attorney with whom we spoke reported that courts do not vigorously enforce the disclosure requirements. If a case has not settled, a judge might warn a plaintiffs' attorney that if he or she does not comply with the case management order the trial will be delayed.

### Admissibility of Trust Claims

The judge reserves the right to determine whether a trust claim is admissible. A plaintiffs' attorney interviewed for the study said that, since the issuance of the March 2010 case management order, he was unaware of any case that had progressed to the point at which defendants requested that claim forms be admitted into evidence. One defense attorney observed that not many defense attorneys have so far requested that trust claim forms be admitted into evidence.

### Setoff Provisions

Plaintiffs are required to disclose all settlements paid in consideration of the injury at issue. Payments must be disclosed regardless of whether the settling party has been found liable, and payments by trusts are treated the same as payments by any other party. The verdict defendants receive pro tanto setoffs for all payments.[57] The court can require the plaintiff to disclose "the amount received or reasonably expected to be received" from trusts or any settling defendant.[58] According to a plaintiffs' attorney who practices in West Virginia, settlements are disclosed post-verdict. One defense attorney interpreted the March 2010 addition to the case management order to mean that a defendant would not have to pay a verdict until a plaintiff had "fully developed" trust claims against viable trusts. The defendant would expect a setoff for the amount that could reasonably expected to be recovered from the trusts. The plaintiff would

---

[55] *In re Asbestos Personal Injury Litigation*, 2010. Emphasis added.

[56] *In re Asbestos Personal Injury Litigation*, 2010.

[57] *Board of Educ.*, 1990; *Smith*, 1993 (citing *Cline*, 1990). See also the discussion in Shelley, Cohn, and Arnold, 2008, p. 268.

[58] *In re Asbestos Personal Injury Litigation*, 2010.

then pursue the trust claims. Whether or not a court would adopt this interpretation remains to be seen.

### Indirect Claims

All unpaid and not-yet-submitted trust claims are assigned to the defendants when a verdict is entered. The case management order directs the plaintiff "to cooperate with and assist the defendants in obtaining damages due and owing to claimant from each asbestos trust as provided by each trust's trust distribution procedures." However, the case management order does not specify what types of assistance are expected and does not provide sanctions for failure to comply. One defense attorney interpreted the requirement for assistance to mean that the plaintiffs' attorney would bring the trust claims. The plaintiff would then keep any payment if the defendant had already received a setoff for the expected trust payment and turn over the payment to the defendant if there had been no setoff. How the case management order regarding indirect claims will be implemented will not become clear until a case has proceeded through entry of the verdict.

# Glossary

**asbestos personal injury trusts.** All trusts created as a result of reorganizations under Chapter 11 of the U.S. Bankruptcy Code, including but not limited to those created pursuant to Section 524(g), that are intended to provide compensation to qualifying claimants alleging personal injury due to asbestos exposure.

**claim form.** The initial documentation required to bring a direct trust claim to an asbestos personal injury trust. We do not use this term to include the trusts' internal work product or any potential settlement offer extended to a claimant.

**crafting a verdict.** See *verdict molding*.

**direct trust claim.** An asbestos trust claim filed by the individual alleging the asbestos-related personal injury or by the individual's attorney on the individual's behalf.

**economic damages.** Tort damages for financial loss suffered consequent to an injury. Examples include wage loss, lost profits, and medical payments. These damages are awarded not as compensation for the harm itself but as compensation for the out-of-pocket financial losses that resulted from the harm.

**indirect trust claim.** A claim for compensation filed with a trust by a party other than the direct claimant. For example, a claim by a verdict defendant for contribution.

**joint-and-several liability.** When liability is joint and several, any and all of the joint tortfeasors can be held liable for the entirety of the plaintiff's injury. The plaintiff need only sue a single joint tortfeasor, regardless of that tortfeasor's relative share of the alleged harm. In some modified joint-and-several-liability states, joint liability attaches only when a defendant's relative share of fault is above an established threshold.

**judgment.** A court's final resolution of a case. For the purposes of this monograph, we use this term to refer to the amount of damages a verdict defendant must pay the plaintiff. Such a defendant is said to "take a judgment," or the court is said to "enter a judgment."

**liquidated value.** The monetary value a trust assigns to an injury, according to a matrix listed in the trust distribution procedures.

**named defendant.** A party named by a plaintiff in an asbestos lawsuit or against which a cross-claim is filed by a party that the plaintiff has named.

**noneconomic damages.** Tort damages awarded for the subjective nonpecuniary harms suffered consequent to an injury. Examples include pain, suffering, and loss of consortium.

**payment percentage.** A percentage applied to the liquidated value that a trust assigns to a claim to determine the amount that will actually be paid to the claimant. Payment percentages are initially set during trust formation but can be changed with the consent of the trust advisory committee and the future claimants' representative.

**pro rata setoff.** A reduction in a verdict equal to the percentage of a joint tortfeasor's share of liability (regardless of the amount actually paid). When liability is joint and several, a pro rata setoff is often equal to the verdict amount divided by the number of parties found liable.

**pro tanto setoff.** A dollar-for-dollar reduction in a verdict for money received from settled parties or trusts (regardless of the joint tortfeasor's share of liability).

**reorganized debtor.** The legal entity that is created on the effective date of a reorganization plan that has been confirmed by the court overseeing the debtor's Chapter 11 bankruptcy case.

**setoff.** See *pro rata setoff* and *pro tanto setoff*.

**several liability.** When liability is several, a defendant is responsible only for the proportion of the fault assigned to it by the trier of fact.

**single-satisfaction state.** A legal jurisdiction that permits a plaintiff to recover once, and only once, the full monetary value for an alleged harm.

**trust distribution procedures.** The document that describes the process by which trust claims will be collected, reviewed, and paid.

**verdict defendant.** A named defendant in a tort action that is found liable to the plaintiff for the alleged harm at the conclusion of a trial. The verdict defendant is responsible for paying the judgment (or a fraction thereof) to the plaintiff.

**verdict molding.** The process of reducing a verdict to reflect money a plaintiff has already received from, for example, settled defendants and trusts. Verdict molding is driven by state law that determines whether setoffs are pro rata, pro tanto, or some blended version.

**verdict sheet.** A form provided to the jury that lists all the parties the jury should consider in assigning fault for the alleged injury even if the parties did not formally appear at trial.

# References

American Academy of Actuaries, Mass Torts Subcommittee, *Overview of Asbestos Claims Issues and Trends*, Washington, D.C., August 2007.

*Andaloro v. Armstrong World Indus.*, 2002 PA Super 112, 799 A.2d 71, April 17, 2002.

Armstrong World Industries Asbestos Trust, *Amended and Restated Armstrong World Industries, Inc., Asbestos Personal Injury Settlement Trust Distribution Procedures*, May 6, 2008, conformed copy reflecting changes made by the first amendment to the amended and restated trust distribution procedures dated July 14, 2010. As of July 11, 2011: http://www.armstrongworldasbestostrust.com/files/Conformed%20AWI%20TDP%20as%20of%207_14_10.PDF

*Baker v. AC&S, Inc.*, 562 Pa. 290, 755 A.2d 664, June 26, 2000.

Baron, Steve, testimony, "Hearing on RTPs," *In re Asbestos Litigation*, District Court, Harris County, Texas, 11th Judicial District, October 16, 2008.

Baron and Budd, "Preparing for Your Deposition," undated.

*Board of Educ. v. Zando, Martin & Milstead, Inc.*, 182 W. Va. 597, 390 S.E.2d 796, February 22, 1990.

*Borel v. Fibreboard Paper Products Corp.*, 493 F.2d 1076, 5th Cir., May 13, 1973.

*Borg-Warner Corp. v. Flores*, 232 S.W.3d 765, June 8, 2007.

California Civil Code, Division 3, Obligations, Part 1, Obligations in general, Title 2, Interpretation of obligations, Chapter 2, Joint or several obligations, Section 1431, Joint liability.

———, Division 3, Obligations, Part 1, Obligations in general, Title 2, Interpretation of obligations, Chapter 2, Joint or several obligations, Section 1431.1, Findings and declaration of purpose.

———, Division 3, Obligations, Part 1, Obligations in general, Title 2, Interpretation of obligations, Chapter 2, Joint or several obligations, Section 1431.2, Several liability for noneconomic damages.

California Code of Civil Procedure, Part 2, Of civil actions, Title 8, Of the trial and judgment in civil actions, Chapter 4, Trial by jury, Article 3, The verdict.

———, Part 2, Of civil actions, Title 11, Contribution among joint judgment debtors, Chapter 1, Releases from and contribution among joint tortfeasors.

———, Part 4, Miscellaneous provisions, Title 4, Civil Discovery Act, Chapter 2, Scope of discovery, Article 1, General provisions, Section 2017.010, What matters may be subject to discovery.

California Evidence Code, Division 9, Evidence affected or excluded by extrinsic policies, Chapter 3, Other evidence affected or excluded by extrinsic policies, Section 1152, Admissibility of evidence of offer to compromise.

———, Division 9, Evidence affected or excluded by extrinsic policies, Chapter 3, Other evidence affected or excluded by extrinsic policies, Section 1154, Offer to discount a claim.

*Canella v. Abex et al.*, court transcript, Supreme Court of the State of New York, County of New York, before Judge Shirley Werner Kornreich, January 24, 2008.

Carroll, Stephen J., Deborah R. Hensler, Jennifer Gross, Elizabeth M. Sloss, Matthias Schonlau, Allan Abrahamse, and J. Scott Ashwood, *Asbestos Litigation*, Santa Monica, Calif.: RAND Corporation, MG-162-ICJ, 2005. As of June 22, 2011: http://www.rand.org/pubs/monographs/MG162.html

Cassada, Garland S., Robinson Bradshaw and Hinson, personal communication, March 7, 2011.

Celotex Trust, *First Amended and Restated Asbestos Settlement Trust Agreement*, Annex B: *Fourth Amended and Restated Asbestos Personal Injury Claims Resolution Procedures*, c. 2008. As of July 11, 2011: http://www.celotextrust.com/files/FourthAmendedPICLAIMSRESOLUTIONPROCEDURES.PDF

*Cline v. White*, 183 W. Va. 43, 393 S.E.2d 923, May 21, 1990.

*Crowell v. City of Phila.*, 531 Pa. 400, 613 A.2d 1178, June 17, 1992.

*DaFonte v. Up-Right, Inc.*, 2 Cal. 4th 593, 828 P.2d 140, May 4, 1992.

*Davies v. Superior Court*, 36 Cal. 3d 291, 682 P.2d 349, July 2, 1984.

Dixon, Lloyd, Geoffrey McGovern, and Amy Coombe, *Asbestos Bankruptcy Trusts: An Overview of Trust Structure and Activity with Detailed Reports on the Largest Trusts*, Santa Monica, Calif.: RAND Corporation, TR-872-ICJ, 2010. As of June 22, 2011: http://www.rand.org/pubs/technical_reports/TR872.html

Dore, Laurie Kratky, "Secrecy by Consent: The Use and Limits of Confidentiality in the Pursuit of Settlement," *Notre Dame Law Review*, Vol. 74, January 1999, p. 283, 1999.

Eggen, Jean M., "Understanding State Contribution Laws and Their Effects on the Settlement of Mass Tort Actions," *Texas Law Review*, Vol. 73, 1995, p. 1701, 1995.

Erichson, Howard M., "A Typology of Aggregate Settlements," *Notre Dame Law Review*, Vol. 80, May 2005, p. 1769.

*Garcia v. Duro Dyne Corp.*, 156 Cal. App. 4th 92, 67 Cal. Rptr. 3d 100, October 16, 2007.

*Glenfed Dev. Corp. v. Superior Court*, 53 Cal. App. 4th 1113, 62 Cal. Rptr. 2d 195, March 27, 1997.

*Greenleaf v. Garlock, Inc.*, 174 F.3d 352, 3d Cir., May 6, 1999.

*Hessong v. AC&S [Warfield]*, case 24X06000460, transcript of pretrial hearings before Judge John M. Glynn, Circuit Court for Baltimore City, January 11, 2011.

Illinois Compiled Statutes Annotated, Chapter 735, Civil procedure, Article II, Civil practice, Part 11, Trial, Section 1116, Limitation on recovery in tort actions.

———, Chapter 735, Civil procedure, Article II, Civil practice, Part 11, Trial, Section 5/2-1118, Exceptions.

———, Chapter 740, Civil liabilities, Joint Tortfeasor Contribution Act, Section 100/2, Right of contribution.

Illinois Rules of Evidence, Article IV, Relevancy and its limits. As of July 18, 2011: http://www.state.il.us/court/SupremeCourt/Evidence/Evidence.htm#Article_IV

Illinois Supreme Court Rules, Article II, Rules on civil proceedings, Part E, Discovery, requests for admission, and pretrial procedure, Rule 201, General discovery provisions. As of July 18, 2011: http://www.state.il.us/court/supremecourt/rules/Art_II/ArtII.htm#201

*In re ACandS Inc.*, case 02-12687 (JKF), Chapter 11, Bankr. Del., May 6, 2008.

*In re all asbestos litigation filed in Madison County*, Circuit Court, Third Judicial Circuit, Madison County, Ill., January 2011. As of July 11, 2011: http://www.co.madison.il.us/circuitclerk/PDF/AsbestosRevisedStandingOrderJan2011.pdf

*In re Asbestos Litigation*, Court of Common Pleas, Philadelphia County, October Term 1986, No. 0001, order of Judge Sandra M. Moss, April 5, 2010.

*In re Asbestos Personal Injury Litigation*, order of Judge Ronald E. Wilson, civil action 03-C-9600, Circuit Court of Kanawha County, W. Va., March 3, 2010.

*In re New York City Asbestos Litigation*, Defendants' Standard Article 16 Interrogatories and Request for Production of Documents, August 27, 2003. As of July 18, 2011: http://www.nycal.net/PDFs/memos/Memo_082703.pdf

*Jhaveri v. Teitelbaum*, 176 Cal. App. 4th 740, 98 Cal. Rptr. 3d 268, August 12, 2009.

*Kananian v. Lorillard Tobacco Co.*, CV 442750, Ohio Cuyahoga County Com. Pl., January 18, 2007.

Kornhauser, Lewis A., and Richard L. Revesz, "Apportioning Damages Among Potentially Insolvent Actors," *Journal of Legal Studies*, Vol. 19, No. 2, June 1990, pp. 617–651.

*Kotler v. Monticello Hospital*, 56 Misc. 2d 742, 290 N.Y.S.2d 385, Supreme Court of New York, Special Term, Queens County, May 1, 1968.

Levy, Marc, "Pennsylvania Governor Signs 'Fair Share' Civil Liability Reform," *Insurance Journal*, June 28, 2011. As of July 22, 2011: http://www.insurancejournal.com/news/east/2011/06/28/204334.htm

*Louk v. Isuzu Motors*, 198 W. Va. 250, 479 S.E.2d 911, December 6, 1996.

*Lundy v. Masson*, 260 S.W.3d 482, Ct. App. Texas, 14th District, Houston, April 29, 2008.

Manville Personal Injury Settlement Trust, *2002 Trust Distribution Process*, January 2010 revision. As of March 4, 2011: http://www.claimsres.com/documents/MT/TDP02.pdf

*Morningstar v. Black & Decker Mfg. Co.*, 162 W. Va. 857, 253 S.E.2d 666, April 13, 1979.

New York Civil Practice Law and Rules, Article 16, Limited liability of persons jointly liable, Section 1601, Limited liability of persons jointly liable. As of July 18, 2011: http://public.leginfo.state.ny.us/LAWSSEAF.cgi?QUERYTYPE=LAWS+&QUERYDATA=$$CVP1601$$@TXCVP01601+&LIST=LAW+&BROWSER=BROWSER+&TOKEN=40983283+&TARGET=VIEW

New York General Obligations, Article 15, Modification and discharge of obligations, Title 1, Discharge of joint obligors, Section 15-108, Release or covenant not to sue. As of July 18, 2011: http://public.leginfo.state.ny.us/LAWSSEAF.cgi?QUERYTYPE=LAWS+&QUERYDATA=$$GOB15-108$$@TXGOB015-108+&LIST=LAW+&BROWSER=BROWSER+&TOKEN=45215335+&TARGET=VIEW

*Nolan v. Weil-McLain*, WL 1012147, Ill., 2009.

*N.Y. City Asbestos Litig. v. A.C. &S.*, 194 Misc. 2d 214, 750 N.Y.S.2d 469, December 17, 2002, aff'd. 775 N.Y.S. 2d 520, 1st Dep't., 2004.

*Ottavio v. Fibreboard Corp.*, 421 Pa. Super. 284, 617 A.2d 1296, December 16, 1992.

Owens Corning Fibreboard Asbestos Personal Injury Trust, OC Sub-Account, *Release and Indemnity Agreement*, undated.

———, *Asbestos Personal Injury Trust Distribution Procedures*, revised February 2, 2010.

Pace, Nick, Seth Seabury, and Arvin Jain, *After the Jury Has Left the Courtroom: Posttrial Changes to Civil Verdicts*, Santa Monica, Calif.: RAND Corporation, draft, 2011.

*Parchefsky v. Kroll Bros., Inc.*, 267 N.Y. 410, 196 N.E. 308, Ct. App. N.Y., May 21, 1935.

*Pennington v. Bluefield Orthopedics, P.C.*, 187 W. Va. 344, 419 S.E.2d 8, Supreme Ct. App. W. Va., June 11, 1992.

Pennsylvania Consolidated Statutes, Title 42, Judiciary and judicial procedure, Part VII, Civil actions and proceedings, Chapter 71, General provisions, Section 7102, Comparative negligence. As of July 18, 2011:
http://www.legis.state.pa.us/WU01/LI/LI/CT/HTM/42/00.071.002.000..HTM

———, Title 42, Judiciary and judicial procedure, Part VII, Civil actions and proceedings, Chapter 83, Particular rights and immunities, Subchapter B, Contribution among tortfeasors, Section 8322, definition. As of July 18, 2011:
http://www.legis.state.pa.us/cfdocs/legis/LI/consCheck.cfm?txtType=HTM&ttl=42&div=0&chpt=83&sctn=22&subsctn=0

———, Title 42, Judiciary and judicial procedure, Part VII, Civil actions and proceedings, Chapter 83, Particular rights and immunities, Subchapter B, Contribution among tortfeasors, Section 8324, Right of contribution. As of July 18, 2011:
http://www.legis.state.pa.us/cfdocs/legis/LI/consCheck.cfm?txtType=HTM&ttl=42&div=0&chpt=83&sctn=24&subsctn=0

———, Title 42, Judiciary and judicial procedure, Part VII, Civil actions and proceedings, Chapter 83, Particular rights and immunities, Subchapter B, Contribution among tortfeasors, Section 8325, Effect of judgment. As of July 18, 2011:
http://www.legis.state.pa.us/cfdocs/legis/LI/consCheck.cfm?txtType=HTM&ttl=42&div=0&chpt=83&sctn=25&subsctn=0

*Puller v. AC&S et al.*, case 24-X-02-000023, Circuit Court for Baltimore County, Md., filed January 10, 2002.

*Ready v. United/Goedecke Services*, 2008 WL 5046833, Ill., November 25, 2008.

*Reed v. Allied Signal et al.*, Consolidated Cases 3022 EDA 2010, 3023 EDA 2010, Opinion by Honorable Stephen E. Levin, Court of Common Pleas of Philadelphia County, December 22, 2010.

*Rutherford v. Owens-Illinois*, 16 Cal. 4th 953, 941 P.2d 1203, October 22, 1997.

*Saichek v. Lupa*, 204 Ill. 2d 127, 787 N.E.2d 827, March 20, 2003.

*Sealover v. Carey Canada*, 996 F.2d 42, 3d Cir., June 22, 1993.

Shanley, Michael G., and Mark A. Peterson, *Posttrial Adjustments to Jury Awards*, Santa Monica, Calif.: RAND Corporation, R-3511-ICJ, 1987. As of June 28, 2011:
http://www.rand.org/pubs/reports/R3511.html

Shelley, William P., Jacob C. Cohn, and Joseph A. Arnold, "The Need for Transparency Between the Tort System and Section 524(g) Asbestos Trusts," *Norton Journal of Bankruptcy Law and Practice*, Vol. 17, 2008, pp. 257–295.

*Sitzes v. Anchor Motor Freight*, 169 W. Va. 698, 289 S.E.2d 679, March 23, 1982.

*Smith v. Monongahela Power Co.*, 189 W. Va. 237, 429 S.E.2d 643, April 8, 1993.

*Snyder v. AC&S et al.*, case 24-X-01-001969, Circuit Court for Baltimore City, Md., filed December 7, 2001.

*Taylor v. John Crane, Inc.*, 113 Cal. App. 4th 1063, 6 Cal. Rptr. 3d 695, November 26, 2003.

Texas Civil Practice and Remedies Code Annotated, Title 2, Trial, judgment, and appeal, Subtitle C, Judgments, Chapter 33, Proportionate responsibility, Subchapter B, Contribution, Section 33.012, Amount of recovery. As of June 28, 2011:
http://www.statutes.legis.state.tx.us/Docs/CP/htm/CP.33.htm

*Thibeault v. Allis Chalmers Corp. Product Liability Trust*, order of the Court of Common Pleas of Montgomery County, Pa., William J. Furber Jr., J., February 22, 2010.

*Volkswagen of America, Inc. v. Superior Court*, 139 Cal. App. 4th 1481, 43 Cal. Rptr. 3d 723, May 26, 2006.

West Virginia Code, Chapter 55, Actions, suits and arbitration, judicial sale, Article 7, Actions for injuries, Section 55-7-24, Apportionment of damages. As of June 28, 2011:
http://www.legis.state.wv.us/WVCODE/Code.cfm?chap=55&art=7

*Wilson v. AC&S et al.*, case 24-X-01-000916, Circuit Court for Baltimore County, Md., filed August 1, 2001